CRYING GIRL

CRYING GIRL

Yvonne Brown

Crying Girl

First Edition
ISBN: 978-1-7336973-0-9
Ebook ISBN: 978-1-7336973-1-6
Jacket Design by Deanna Deley
Back-of-Jacket photograph by Brandon Gerald

For my mother, Nusrat,
and my daughters, Layla and Samira

"I remember you. You're the Crying Girl."

—Toni Morrison
Northern Kentucky University
July 2005

Dear President Carter,
Here's to Living the American Dream
God Bless you and your family
2/2020

A camel stumbles around a mountain's lip. A mini-skirt is planted on amorous olive hips while a woman's eyes seduce a man outside. A beggar pushes his shopping cart down a narrow, busy street shouting, "Coats! ... Pants! ... Sweaters!" Little children whose eyebrows are larger than themselves scramble for pomegranates at Tehran's Grand Bazaar. Trucks, vans, and motorcycles fight to get through a sidewalk masquerading as a "street." Not one accident happens even though children playfully weave between cars. Boiling parsley perfumes the air. That is my image of Iran. That is the Iran I see; a land oceans away. As years pass, the world has become smaller, the oceans wider. Like a child standing at the edge of a pool, waiting to jump into the arms of a loving parent, I fear returning to Iran. The place where my grandparents are buried, a land where half of my identity exists. My mother's land.

PART ONE

CHAPTER ONE

A memo from my supervisor stated that I would conduct a computer operating training to a new staff of thirty-five personnel in two weeks on February 27, 1976. What the memo left out were two facts: except for me, the staff would be all male and from a team of five American men, I, Nusrat Rahimi, was the most qualified for the job.

On the corner of Takte Tavoose Avenue, less than two miles north of the American Embassy, I worked for the Imperial Iranian Navy Advanced Accounting Consultants, sub-contracted under Honeywell. Constructed under the modernization program initiated by the Shah, the five-story brick office building stood firm as a symbol of Iran's growing stature. "I'm up for the challenge," I affirmed aloud from my cubicle after sharing the news with my parents over the phone. As I prepared to leave for the day, I gathered my notebook and a folder of memos and placed them in my brown leather attaché. Grabbing my coat, I headed out the door.

I had earned a bachelor's degree in history from Tehran University and had received a certificate from Controlled Data IBM in London. My education and command of both English and Farsi did, in fact, make me highly qualified for the job. At 26, never did I imagine my beauty or my family's position among the religious elite would sway things in my favor. And while these points didn't hinder any good fortune that came my way, I always attributed my upward mobility to hard work having paid off instead of privilege.

When I left the office building, I caught a cab parked in front of the entrance among a lineup of some four dozen other cars waiting to pick people up as they got off work. As my cab headed north, a thick grey sky outlined the varying heights of buildings. Soon the city would be left behind. A storm had been predicted which meant the winter's first snow would fall at any moment. The endless panorama of the Alborz Mountain faded into the oncoming night. Along the roadside were a few bare trees and the bazaar. A stray dog roamed the streets. My heart struck a note of grief at how the dog resembled my Gooshi.

As a child, I had secretly adopted a wayward dog. During the day, the dog slunk through the streets, eventually making his way to my back door by dusk. He came in knowing he was outlawed, that the possibility of someone finding out about him would mean his imminent execution. I felt sorry for this outcast. Considered filthy beasts carrying diseases, dogs were forbidden in my family. It was a sin to bring them into the home or show them preferential treatment. The dog's blindness only made me more sympathetic. Although his gray, opaque eyes were useless, his long coyote-like ears served as guides to his survival. His presence became living proof of the miracles of an unseen power. If he could continue to exist and was sent to me, then it was somehow divine. Though he looked old and slovenly, I saw the beauty in his mangy coat. In my eyes, he was sprightly as a pup.

I vowed to keep my dear friend alive, despite the powers who were bent on eradicating creatures like him. For four long weeks, I secretly set aside scraps saved from family meals to give to my Gooshi. For the first time, the isolation I felt as a child subsided.

I remembered the day I walked home from the schoolhouse. The sun seemed to brighten as if I had somehow been given a sacred role in controlling the light. With my books in tow, I hummed a silent prayer.

Then came a horrible howling intermingled with eerily wild cackling. The noise drew me off my usual path home, and my feet felt compelled to follow until I came to a tin house outside the marketplace. The voices became much more than distant mumbled ranting and had transformed into what sounded like sadistic proclamations. The clamor was all too familiar.

I saw several neighborhood boys dragging my Gooshi through the streets beyond the tin house behind the marketplace. Some of them taunted the dog while others threw stones. The boys had tied him to a post and decided to stage a makeshift execution. It appeared ritualistic with Gooshi as the sacrificed savior. I'll never forget how he seemed to look at me with his blind eyes. I felt he could see through my soul. There was nothing I could do because my love for him was forbidden. I thought I had betrayed my only friend. That regret was forever etched in my psyche. Even worse, some of the boys would later become my family-appointed suitors.

Grounded in generations of religious clerics, I came from a respectable family in Tehran. While Baba, my father, was a man of high moral standing, he didn't follow the path of becoming an Ayatollah like his father but instead worked in the booming oil industry. We lived in a large house in Davoodiyeh, a prestigious neighborhood in northern Tehran built exclusively for National Iranian Oil Company personnel and their families. When my father purchased the property in the late sixties, there was more prestige and higher status in working for the oil company than in working for the state department or the military. Far away from onlookers and guarded at night by a security officer, the new residential area was near Sadabad, a five-minute drive from one of the Shah's summer homes.

The cab went down Mir Damad Lane, turned left on Pahlavi Street, and finally stopped at Twenty-Three Oil Lane. Encased in white marble, the two-story apartment was built on undeveloped farmland and had the feel of 1970's nouveau. However, it stayed true to Iranian architecture which included a garden, courtyard, and veranda. It was a beautiful marriage between nature and our little heaven on Earth.

Recently, Amir, the gardener, had meticulously placed an array of tulip bulbs around the base of the marble fountain in the backyard. This was a man who planted as if he were a mother hen tending to her cherished flock. With a mixture of love and artistry, Amir's arrangements exuded life. With each spring my family looked forward to the blooming of his artistry. Someone looking closely at Amir's work-worn eyes and physique might conclude it was not merely a duty, but a representation of all that was transcendent in his life. During the spring, Amir ensured all the plants were hydrated. But now, in the middle of winter, he had put them away in the basement, where fully-lit windows faced the backyard.

When I got home, I walked down the hallway heading towards my room. I heard Maman, my mother, bragging over the phone with Auntie Aziz, her youngest sister. "Yes, Nusrat is a fantastic cook. I trained her well."

There was no dramatic entrance or concern that I would interrupt Maman's phone call. I came home at the same time every day and understood what I was expected to do. My mother was lying on the couch in the living room, smoking a cigarette with one hand and holding the receiver in the other. At thirty-nine, she was thirteen years older than me and twenty years younger than my father. Her skin was an even olive color. Her hair was thick and shiny black with a red tint that was best seen in direct sunlight. Maman rolled her hair every night except on Mondays when she conditioned her scalp with mustard oil. Her hair and eyebrows were her prized attributes. Luckily, she passed them on to me.

I smiled at Maman and kissed her on the cheek.

"Yes, Aziz, Nusrat just arrived." She lowered the receiver, covering it with her hand, "Hello Nusrat Joon." Maman whispered.

I winked, signaling my delight, and went to my room. Recently, I had played a part in reconciling the two sisters. They had been estranged for a year. No one in the family knew why they were fighting, even the sisters themselves. So here they were again, arguing about nothing like they did before their big fight. It was their pastime, a ritual to prove who ran their households best or who was more beautiful. Ordinarily, the sisters' quarreling was something that would upset the entire family. But with time my father and I, and the extended family grew to accept the nature of these hot-blooded sisters who would have had their tongues cut out before speaking a kind word to one another.

As I walked into my room, Maman's voice could still be heard throughout the house: "It's the least Nusrat can do since she isn't married yet. We would love to have some grandchildren before we hit the grave."

I paused and shook my head, anticipating the upcoming onslaught of Maman's disappointment. I took a deep breath, released it, and laid down my attaché. I hurriedly changed into my housedress because I had to get dinner ready so my father would have something to eat when he arrived at 7:00 p.m. I closed the bedroom door behind me and made my way to the kitchen. Maman, who often fell victim to depression and did nothing but complain about it, passed by. She reminded me not to burn the tahdig, crunchy rice from the bottom of the pot.

"And you should prepare the henna tonight," she said. "Have you *looked* in the mirror lately?"

"What's wrong with my hair Maman? I've rolled it every night."

"No, you have to give it shine."

"I'm fine with my hair. If you want me to fix it, that's what you should have said to begin with. Not all this business that my hair doesn't look nice."

"How do you expect to marry if you don't care for your hair?" Maman asked. "Prepare the henna *tonight*, don't delay anymore."

The topics of my hair and marriage were Maman's way to pick at me bit by bit. Why couldn't she be satisfied with how far I had come in my education and job instead? Maman hung up the phone, and I seized the opportunity to get a word in. "I wish you understood how much I have on my mind with work. I'm not thinking about a husband right now."

"What's wrong with you? You're beautiful and smart," she motioned with her hand from my face to my waistline. "So what if you are a little fat. Some men like it. Isn't anyone expressing interest in you? Everyone that comes to us for your hand, you don't want. I got married at eleven, a suitable age to have babies and take care of the home. What's your issue Nusrat? You didn't even want Babak Alijan. And he was the first Iranian pilot! I don't understand it. You need to wake up. There will come a day when you will be too old, your beauty gone, and you'll have nothing but memories of all the men you turned away. What use will this be to you or *me?* "

"Maybe I have someone suitable in mind," I said, teasing Maman.

Her eyebrows jumped and I knew she was dying to hear more.

"Have you ever stopped to think that I was waiting to see what Allah wants for me?" I knew Maman wanted to push it further, to get one more word in.

"Just fix the henna and we'll see what happens," she said.

Irritated, I headed to the kitchen to prepare dinner. Washing my hands in the sink, I saw the sun had finally disappeared behind the mountains. I could see my face in the dark window. It was true what everyone had said, I was a younger version of Maman. But my face looked tired from all I had to do for myself, Maman and the household. And yet, I felt wiser than my age, ahead of my time and confident in my future.

I closed the curtains and retrieved a bag of henna powder from the cabinet. I set it aside. Then I pulled the bowl of thawed ghormeh sabzi from the refrigerator and poured its contents into a pot. Soon, the food sizzled, so I added a little water. It was 5:30 p.m. and I wanted to make sure the rice had enough time to cook. Calculating how long it would take to make tahdig, I gently stirred the food so as not to bruise the kidney beans.

Like my parents, I enjoyed the crunch from the tahdig. My Auntie Aziz often reminded me of an old wives' tale: "If you eat tahdig too much, it will rain on your wedding day."

I would laugh, marriage was far from my mind. If I stopped eating tahdig, it would be to manage my waistline, not for how it might affect the weather on my wedding day. Besides, that day wasn't coming any time soon.

I grabbed the bowl of rice that I had soaked the night before. I half boiled it, and then drained it in a colander. Spooning out a tiny amount to taste, I was pleased it wasn't salty. In the background, I could hear Maman babbling to Auntie Aziz again. Her raspy voice rose and at times changed to screaming. When she was in the midst of one of her explosive pity parties, it would always be about the same things. "No one has suffered more than me. My husband divorced me. Then we married again. He fools around with women who smile in my face. I want to give him a son. Allah only knows if he already has one that nobody knows about with some animal somewhere in the Alborz Mountains."

Although I was used to Maman's complaints, they never ceased to annoy me. Sometimes I wanted to beg her to "shut up," but I wouldn't dare.

Whether Baba cheated on her or not was a mystery. No one had ever caught him. Why would they? Everyone loved him because he knew how to make people feel valued. Once, one of the servants told me, "I love Mr. Rahimi and I feel expensive in his presence."

From servants to high-ranking officials, no one was immune to Baba's charm. He was so likable that even if he had engaged in adultery or some other inappropriate behavior, the witness would deny what their eyes had seen. Their mouths would remain shut.

I retrieved the bag of henna and poured it into a medium bowl. Sprinkling in a little cinnamon and clove powder, I added water and mixed it into a paste. I could mix henna and apply it without making a mess, something I learned to do as a child. I knew Maman respected this skill, but I wished I could forget the feelings that came to me every time I prepared it: the pain of my parents divorcing when I was seven years old, Maman crying, and then moving to Bombay in search of Baba.

And yet, listening to Maman on the phone as I walked through the kitchen, I had to admit that in the chaos of my parents' home, I had ideas that I had to keep to myself. Plans that may have made Maman, with her bursts of emotional highs and lows, believe it was reasonable to pray for death.

My parents were the first to ever divorce in the family which was why I wasn't rushing to get married. Keeping this to myself, I could never let these thoughts come out in an argument. As a child, I played with my dolls, often imagining the husband and wife were loving. I had hoped that whenever Maman grew angry at Baba for leaving us, she would cling to me and transform her pain into love. Sometimes when Maman was angry with Baba, she would tell me it was not my fault that he left. I wanted her to sit and play with me, perhaps show me with dolls that a husband and wife could love each other. Never would Maman rip apart the husband doll when I asked for Baba and scream, "Forget this doll and forget Baba!"

When my parents divorced, Baba left us in Iran and started an import/export business in Bombay. In the midst of experiencing difficulty with the sharp transitions of my parent's decisions, at just eight-years-old, I learned about henna from a servant. Baba was chasing money, and Maman was chasing him until they remarried. Even then, Maman was fearful and insecure in their second marriage. It didn't matter if he was in Iran or Bombay, women and men were equally drawn to him. Sometimes he seemed to relish excessively over the attention.

I was quite amazed by how Baba saw himself. He often said, "The people like me because of who my father is, not because I'm great or so and so." Perhaps what saddened Maman the most was that she wanted to give him more children. Even now, I thought, Maman would have another baby if she could. The possibility of this not happening at Maman's age brought me some relief. I knew she would make me raise the baby.

As it was, I was Maman's anchor in the midst of whatever storm she created. As far as I could remember, she believed Baba had remarried her for my sake. Did Allah soften his heart on account of me despite the complexities that came from their twenty-year age difference? I'm not sure, but I liked to hear Maman tell that story even now, for I saw that I was something wonderful between them. And yet, it was as if Maman had decided she was going to get back at me for something we both wanted: our family being together.

Growing up, I was spoiled with fancy clothes and one-on-one attention from my grandparents and other relatives. Even still, I spent many days and nights feeling isolated as I resented Maman for making me her caretaker. In a way, she held me hostage emotionally with threats like: "You're my daughter. If you don't take care of me, I will die. Do you want your mother to die?" And then there was the wrath Maman would inflict on me when she suspected Baba's infidelity: "I have to take care of you while Baba is doing whatever he wants and while I'm *sick*!"

The pain I endured through Maman's out-of-control behavior made me vow to never be like her. With no one to turn to, I kept her behavior a secret, guarding her against being shamed by the family. As a result, I felt alienated from her and our family, especially when I needed them the most. When Maman's season of depression was over, and she once again felt youthful and energetic, she customarily dropped me with an auntie or my grandparents for weeks on end for no particular reason, except to make me long for her more. I was glad when my parents remarried, but Maman's ways, on top of adjusting to life in Bombay, proved difficult: learning a new language, meeting new servants, and adapting to a new diet was exhausting. One benefit that came from this long-term cruelty was that it ultimately prepared me for attending school many years later in London. The further away I was from my mother, the easier it was to breathe. Overcome with homesickness, I finished my two-year program in eighteen months eager to return home once again.

At this point, my parent's marriage had been steady for years. It was almost like the divorce had never happened, just a small bump on life's road. I covered the bowl of henna with a cloth, and just like that, I heard Maman shift from expressing her miseries to boasting.

"Yes, today my husband sent a letter directly to the king himself, updating him on the progress of the oil company," or "My husband is begging me to relax my mind and go shopping at the boutiques in Abbas Abad," or "I have full authority over my husband's checkbook, he has to ask me for the money," or her latest boast, "Nusrat has a high rank at her computer job. She's so useful with the computer that she's going to train others."

Hearing Maman's last sentence, I chuckled. Then my mood quickly changed when I heard her yelling: "Did you fix the henna as I told you? Will the food be ready in time for Baba?"

"Yes, Maman," I responded as I secured the kitchen cloth around the pot and covered it with the lid. "It will be ready when Baba comes home."

At least I could help Maman. At least she was receiving care from a loving daughter who wasn't yet a wife. But deep down, I knew Maman was okay with me not being married. If I were married, she wouldn't have me all to herself. Her words were a show. She was the actress, my aunties, her audience. I went to my room and pulled out my Controlled Data book. Blocking out all the distractions in my head, I studied for hours in preparation for my training session.

CHAPTER TWO

Two weeks went by. I felt fully prepared for the training session where I was to communicate with the Iranian staff in Farsi about the company's movement towards technological advancement. Eager to begin, I welcomed the challenge of having an audience of men who couldn't even pronounce the word "computer." Yes, some soldiers got the job because of their advanced math skills, but I imagined most of them got their positions through some high-powered relative. Curtis Brown, my American counterpart, sat in on my session and appeared anxious to hear me speak. "As you know, payroll is currently done manually," I said after introducing myself to the group. "This approach is no longer considered satisfactory in meeting the military's goals of reliable, accurate, and concise productivity."

Glancing at Curtis, I noticed how focused he was on me. *Was he analyzing my every word? I knew he didn't understand my language. What was he thinking?* I continued, "How will we do this? By computerizing payroll."

For a moment, I could tell they were all dazzled by the succinct manner in which I spoke. The idea of a computer seemed marvelous in its potential. Adding me, a woman to the equation probably stirred more curiosity.

"This will not be completed overnight, but I will explain it and guide you through it," I observed their uneasiness. In training myself to elaborate on even the most sophisticated aspects of the computer's capabilities, I was mindful to not overwhelm them with complex details. Admittedly, I didn't want to lose anyone in that moment.

"No worries if it doesn't make sense, it will with time. Our goal is for the computer to calculate payroll data in allocating and distributing various costs among specified departments. Instead of signing in and out, payroll will be monitored on a time card. The challenge will be to make sure the time cards are classified by department to facilitate smooth processing."

Scrutiny was nothing new to me, especially in the workplace. I was used to being the center of intrigue. To be in charge of computer instruction made me a novelty, whether the men knew it or not. I had no problem with their attention, which is why I made every effort to appear secure and firm. Never mind that I'd spent every night reading about computers to prepare for the following day. I couldn't afford not to know something or, even worse, be seen as a joke. I shot another glance at Curtis. He was smiling, hopefully with pride and not from being critical of my instruction. *He kept his eyes on me. There was more to his smile. But what? I felt drawn to him. His eyes, his lips, and how they said more to me than words.* Gathering myself, I carried on with instruction.

"In a few minutes, I will meet you again in the computer room. But before we transition, I want to share something with you that I've never told an American." I paused for a moment. "If man can go to the moon, then Iran can have the best computer too!"

At that, they all rose to their feet clapping except for Curtis, who looked clueless.

A short time later, we entered the computer room. It was like something they had never seen. The big machine before us with lights and buttons everywhere drew excitement like it was one big toy. One of the employees even said, "It looks like an airplane cockpit."

I gave them a moment to take it in, then proceeded with my presentation. "This computer cannot do anything by itself. It works only as well as the information we put into it."

I showed them the card reader, the size of my palm, and drew their attention to the various zeroes and symbols on it. Sliding it into the feeder slot, I said, "This will compute and calculate with impressive accuracy and speed."

I knew he was watching. I felt his eyes on every slight movement my hands made. I wondered if he felt me too. Was he fantasizing about my hands touching his body? Could he imagine me whispering my desires for him in Farsi? We all stood and watched the green and white lights flicker.

"Now, follow me to the printer where we will see what the card reader processed."

When we got to the printer, I saw it was out of paper and almost panicked. "Loading the paper is a process in and of itself. I wasn't prepared to show you this today. But it's nevertheless a teachable moment."

The next day, my supervisor publicly praised me on a great training session. To my amazement, he awarded me with the Employee of the Month plaque and even nicknamed me "Walking Computer." It was thrilling to be recognized for my work. But I knew I was growing at a faster rate than Curtis. What normally took the average person a year to learn, I got in half the time. I did my best, but I couldn't help but notice how hard it was for him to keep up sometimes. Mindful of this, I kept an even posture whenever someone complimented me in his presence. It was obvious that he felt threatened in his position when he stopped training others. It wasn't like he came out and said, "I'm not training anyone else," he just stopped. If this was his way of ensuring job security, I feared it would make him look unfavorable to our superiors. I needed him here. He couldn't just jeopardize his job and respect. *Who else would look at me with those eyes? Who else would dare to undress me without removing my clothes?*

"Good God! This woman is driving me nuts!"

From the back of a small conference room lined with metal folding chairs, Curtis watched Nusrat explain the direction of the company to the new employees. Listening for Farsi words he had already known, he attempted to connect words he was unfamiliar with to make sense in his mind. He hoped he could learn Farsi that way.

Never before had he worked this close to an Iranian woman, or any woman, for that matter. The level at which she had the group of twenty or so personnel's attention was something worthy of a television audience. Though she spoke predominantly in her native tongue, Curtis knew she demonstrated full command of the English language. When they started working together, it didn't take him long to see she was hardly limited in proficiency in the way that he and other Americans had initially expected. Her knowledge of the computer system and its complex technological language was impressive. As the training progressed, he finally perked up. He heard her use a word he knew, "American." Suddenly, the room burst with excitement and everyone clapped for Nusrat.

Just last August, Curtis had initiated the first launch to computerize the Iranian military payroll system. The office staff had worked overtime. As the lead computer operator and the only one with civilian and military expertise, Curtis set up a strategic plan to get the program running. Knowing the magnitude of this project, he strived for error-free payroll production. The task ahead of him was to convert manual payroll practices to a first-ever computerized system as had happened successfully in America. And yet, he feared job loss would result from a payroll mishap. So, he charged Amy, the newly hired secretary from Iowa, with readying the timesheets for the following day. The information needed to compile the timesheets arrived later than usual from the military's central office. The additional pressure to meet the deadline created panic for Curtis and other workers already accustomed to tight timetables.

He reported to work at 6:00 a.m., an hour before his scheduled time. Walking with the frustration, urgency, and stress of someone unsure if he needed sex, sleep, or to punch someone in the face, Curtis grabbed a daily paper from the lobby newsstand. He headed for the elevator to the second floor. Continuing past the empty cubicles, he wondered why he was the only one who showed up early, especially on a Monday morning when final reports were due to the boss. Before he reached his office, Curtis headed for Amy's desk, which sat in the open. To his relief, she was there before he arrived. An average sized woman of about 28 years old, her blond hair attracted many of the Iranian male staff. Curtis observed how she loved them doting on her and how rumor had it that she quickly gave in to sleeping with several of them. He saw how she was visibly distraught as she frantically sorted through stacks of papers in haste. He asked, "What's going on?"

"Oh!" Amy peeped up. "Good morning, Mr. Brown!"

He saw her rummaging through papers and wished she would hurry up and find them so he could get on with his work. Curtis set his eyes on a framed picture of Amy holding a cat and an evil eye knickknack that aroused his distaste for pushy bazaar merchants. He said, "Those folders should be on my desk instead of all over the place here. I expected you to be on top of this."

"I know, Mr. Brown. I'm so sorry. I'll have them ready for you in a few minutes."

"You're missing the point, young lady." He placed his hand on her left shoulder when he wanted to snap her ponytail back. "They should be on my desk *now*!" He pounded his other hand on her desk for impact.

"I'm so sorry, Mr. Brown. I'm on it."

"You're lucky you remind me of one my favorite strippers back home," Curtis said. "But if I don't see them on my desk in the next fifteen minutes, you'll wish you had nine lives like your Morris the cat here." He pointed to her picture and laughed.

And now Nusrat was a hero. Curtis watched all his previous hard work go down the drain to a newly hired employee. His situation was complicated: he had fallen for a woman who could take his job and make him insignificant. And yet her new nickname, "Walking Computer," aroused him so much that he practiced it out loud. This was a kind of torture for him as it stirred mixed feelings of envy and delight.

That night Curtis went to a bowling alley with a couple of his American buddies. He looked forward to the next day when he could find something to discuss with Nusrat besides her greatness at work. First thing in the morning, he saw her sitting at her desk in the computer room. She was busy at work, but when he walked into the room, their eyes met and she smiled. This small act was just the boost his confidence needed to begin talking.

"You know we went to the bowling alley last night. I noticed something weird. Is it alright if I run it by you to get some understanding of it?"

"Sure. What happened?" She put her pen down.

"Well, while we were bowling, I noticed we were the only ones actually bowling. Everyone else was just sitting around socializing. It didn't make sense. Why would they come to a bowling alley and not bowl?"

"That's how we are," Nusrat smiled. "We're social people. Maybe they didn't have the money to bowl. Or maybe they enjoyed learning how to bowl from you, the American professional. We don't bowl, that place was built for you and the French. You don't notice Iranians only run it? They're just enjoying a different place to socialize is all."

"But it seems like they're the same people every time we go bowling. They're just sitting drinking tea and watching us. It's weird. Why aren't they working? They look like they sit there all day like the people on welfare back home."

"*Welfare*? What's that?"

"It's where black people sit, do nothing, and rely on the government to take care of them and all their kids that they keep having out of wedlock."

"It's great that a program like that exists. Here, it's the family's duty, no matter their social or financial class, to help family members in hardship. According to our holy book, it's our responsibility to help. Why do you have such a problem with that? How can this be a bad thing?"

"I don't have a problem with it. I just don't want my hard earned tax money supporting anyone who'd rather sit on their ass than work."

"But if the government doesn't help them, *who* will?"

"Don't know. Don't care. I work hard for mine. They can work hard for theirs. Here's another way to look at it: you're intelligent, educated, hard-working, and a woman on top of all that. You're most impressive, don't you think? And it doesn't hurt that you're also easy on the eyes." He beamed, hoping she noted the compliment. "But that's beside the point. You get what I'm saying, don't you?

"I guess so." Nusrat looked confused.

"Well, I trust your husband gets it."

"You don't see a ring on my finger."

"I didn't want to assume anything. Surely someone like you has at least a boyfriend."

"No, no boyfriend. I'm alone. Just me and my work."

"You mean to tell me that none of the Iranian guys here haven't approached you?"

"They know my family. My grandfathers are well-known Ayatollahs. Not just here, but in Iraq, India, and Pakistan."

"Wow. That's amazing!"

"To some maybe, but, because of this, men are intimidated and reluctant to ask for my hand. They fear that they could never measure up. This is what I've learned, this is what I've come to know."

"Gosh, really, Nusrat?" He noted the opportunity and went in for it. "I'm impressed with how well you communicate. I wish I could get through to people the way you do. Tell me, what do you say that makes them stand and clap?"

Then immediately his view sharpened its focus to the tip of her tongue which flickered as it produced a polite response, "*tanks*" instead of "thanks."

"Your 'tanks' is the best thanks I *ever* heard."

From that moment, he made it his duty to shower her with compliments just to hear her say it. He wondered if she would ever catch on to this or worse be rejected by his new love interest. Then he devised a clever plan to get her attention without looking desperate.

"I'm dying to learn Farsi."

"Really? Are you asking me to teach you? I know all the Americans here are eager to learn. I'm sure you already know how to say all the cuss words. Correct?"

Curtis laughed. "For a brief moment, you reminded me of a third-grade teacher I once had a crush on." Then, he smiled and his face blushed. "But, yes, that would be correct."

"Here's another word for you to add to your Farsi vocabulary. It demands that you make a guttural sound like, "Qha-dah-fiss."

He attempted to mimic the pronunciation with much difficulty. "What does that mean?"

"Good-bye." She laughed and gathered her purse. "Have a good evening Curtis. I don't want to miss my bus."

He had to quickly think and respond, "Why don't we continue this conversation over cocktails?"

Shaking her head "no," she declined. "I don't drink."

As a result of Nusrat's refusal to accompany Curtis in what he considered an after-work excursion instead of a date, his heart grew hungrier for her company. Every day, just short of closing time, he envisioned her accepting his proposal. She would agree to simply have a drink. The two of them would walk hand in hand to the neighboring restaurant. Making a grand entrance to the cheers of familiars who would look to them, a power couple, with a sort of reverence he had never known. But this was only a dream. Now, his eyes followed her as she meticulously prepared herself at 5:00 p.m. for her journey home. He watched the way she neatly organized her paperwork and slid every writing utensil back into its usual formation like tiny soldiers waiting to be commanded back into action the next duty day. He followed her as she walked head high out of the building and stepped majestically onto the bus that became a carriage in his mind. The carriage awaited her arrival with bated breath, for she alone was the sole passenger, to be taken to a palace that he only dared envision.

And so as his dream turned back into reality, Curtis began his trek to the watering hole. Dejected and alone, he met the unyielding dry greeting of the regular barflies, who served to remind him of what appeared to be taboo for him to probably ever know, a love unattainable. On one such day, he met his Iranian friend in the lonely ritual, Abas, who after a few shots at the bar would become a grand philosopher of sorts. "If your heart is heavy, you can give it up, for an Iranian woman of her stature is of the highest standard and hard for an Iranian man to get close to, which therefore means impossible for you, an American."

But today Curtis had an air of being more melancholy than usual and Abas said, "Curtis, I can see it in your eyes that you're in love with this woman and if you truly want to go after her with a pure heart, you must take the necessary steps into a culture unlike what you are used to." He went on, "My sister was with an American and he, like you, expected her to be receptive to the rituals of American relationships. His attempts at what he considered normal were shot down. He viewed her as being cold, but he had no clue and no mentor to guide him into the strict covenant that did not allow for the type of courting you are used to in the states. There is no American-style courting in our culture, no walks in the garden, no light-hearted dinners—only love and marriage. Not being able to accept this, my sister's lover sought the comfort of another whose way of living was more in line with his own and my sister was devastated. You see, she was only following what she knew and he did the same, so in actuality, there was no one at fault. It's simply that culture mixing can be very complicated and to someone like yourself and my sister, brutal."

Curtis' face grew flat in a look of utter despair. In an attempt to give his friend a beacon of light, Abas cautioned, "But there is hope if you are willing to accept what she believes and genuinely commit to trying to understand. Then and only then will you unlock the entrance that is blocking your destiny."

"So what do I do?" Curtis asked his heart heavy with confusion.

"The short answer is simple: marry her. But to get to this point, you have to tread lightly with your best foot forward. I know how it is in America. You can make sex anytime with anybody. But it's just not like that here even though we do have our places, like the New City filled with prostitutes. You must know an unmarried woman like her is probably still a virgin, even though she's old. You have to be sensitive to this point. And always remember, every meeting or social opportunity is always considered a bridge to marriage."

In Nusrat, Curtis thought he found the perfect woman. Previously, he rushed into relationships and even a failed marriage, but he had never experienced the emotion that was blind to class divisions, religious prejudices, and cultural differences. Before his love for Nusrat, he only interacted with women like him: white, American, and Christian. Here in Iran, she was a beauty. With her olive skin, she could pass for a tanned brunette back home. It would be when she spoke that her accent gave her away. Even still, Nusrat was an exception that his heart made and a decision his mind could live with. Ultimately, how was he going to get her?

A She-Camel consecrates her odyssey to the future. A child not yet born sight-sees the parental alter between seen and unseen worlds. Sacred space is created for manifesting love, marriage, and me. I've been on this road before my birth. I'm not supposed to believe in reincarnation.

CHAPTER THREE

The sun had yet to make its full pass over the horizon, and the light breeze of March beckoned Iranians outdoors to celebrate Norouz, the Persian New Year of March 1976. Curtis and James marked James' unexpected promotion over drinks at the local bar. Sitting in the midst of the ever-hovering gray clouds of American cigarettes and Cuban cigars, Curtis masked his jealousy by keeping the rounds of Jack on the rocks and Heineken Dark continuously flowing. James had been on the job working with Curtis for less than six months. Yet, somehow he wrested the promotion from management. That alone made Curtis extremely uneasy. As the spirits caught hold of his sensibilities, Curtis' mind was pervaded with the thought of James' unwitting theft of what Curtis had believed was due to him long ago. He thought of the constant announcement of "Congratulations on your promotion, James" by colleagues who of course also adored Nusrat.

"Enough talk about the job," James put his beer down. "I want to know what's going on with the foxy Iranian girl."

Curtis wondered why James didn't say her name and sensed something wasn't right.

"I see how you guys look at each other." He grinned at Curtis. "Everybody sees it in the office."

"I'm going to make her my wife," Curtis said, aware he caught James off guard.

"Are you guys even dating?

Curtis saw James' half-grin and surveyed his eyes thinking of an appropriate response. He speculated on why James had an interest in him and Nusrat; Curtis concluded James was nothing more than jealous.

"Besides, I don't know if you have a chance."

"Well, I'll be the judge of that," Curtis noted the threat. "You know the women here are raised to listen and make their husbands happy? They're not like American women with all that women's lib shit. I'll have her all to myself. You know, start a life and make some babies. What's it to you anyway?"

"Face it, man, she's educated, she comes from a super-religious family with a lot of pull, and she's too good-looking to be with a guy like you."

"Look buddy," Curtis leaned closer toward James. His eyes tightened, his nostrils flared with indignation, "You're crossing the line now." He paused for a methodically drawn-out second. "It seems to me you know a little too much about my lady."

James threw his hands up as if to show he wasn't armed, "Whoa, Chief." He turned his head in the direction of the bartender. "Barkeep, another round for my colleague." Returning to Curtis, he made solid eye contact. "Easy does it. It's not that serious."

Curtis looked at him intently then checked his watch, "I'm heading out now."

⇥ ⇤

As his peer working in the same department, Curtis treated me with mutual respect. Sure, I knew he could be difficult. I had heard the stories of how he treated his secretary, but I also knew how others talked about him behind his back. James had made it his duty to "protect me from Curtis." *But why*? Poor Curtis was probably bitter feeling alone and misunderstood in a new country. His tough-man exterior was not at all who he was in reality.

We worked well together. I couldn't understand what James had to gain from speaking ill about Curtis. James would preface his information with, "There's a side to him that you don't see and you need to know about."

Why would I need to know about something that had nothing to do with me? I wasn't there, so why was it so important? James told me how he noticed me and Curtis spending more time than usual and wanted me to be okay. Why wouldn't I be okay? Just because people gossiped about Curtis didn't mean he would be that way with me. That was the problem with the world: everyone was worried about what the other person was doing and not focusing on their own damn self. There was more to him. I had seen it when our eyes locked.

Despite James' warning, I kept a professional posture with Curtis. But was I imagining the brief, yet penetrating stares from the computer room? Did I not hear him breathe in my scent? What about the countless moments of catching the other one staring and then carrying on with work? I delighted in the attention so much that the layers of my former reservations peeled away like old skin giving way to new. James had only increased my curiosity. Something told me that his tale was coming from a jealous place. Perhaps this was the push I needed to contemplate the possibilities of Curtis. Maybe I could help him be more trusting? Surely Allah had appointed me to bring comfort and friendship to my colleague. Underneath it all, I knew he was a kind man. By April of 1976, I had known him for eight months, almost a year. Until he asked me out again, I chose to put him in the distance of my mind.

It was midday, on a Wednesday afternoon when we decided to have lunch in the office courtyard. The area was planted with fragrant orange trees. At its center was a turquoise fountain surrounded by the intoxicating scent of lavender potted in terracotta. Beyond this, in the corner of the courtyard, stood a green cast iron bench where Curtis suggested we sit and eat.

Mindful of my figure, I packed a lunch with chicken kabob and cucumber salad. He took a seat and said, "Have I told you today how beautiful you are?"

"Yes, and tanks." I felt a warm sensation of embarrassment come over my face and knew in my heart that I had to be completely red.

"Are *you* blushing?" He smiled. "That's encouraging. I mean, I think you're really amazing."

Sitting next to him, I watched as he methodically pulled out his plate and utensils. I saw Curtis open a small hand-held cooler and wondered what he had brought to eat. After he pulled out his food container, I could tell it was leftovers of ghormeh sabzi. He carefully put his food on a plate. "What happened to your meat?"

"I ate it all last night," he chuckled. "The food at the Takte-Jamshid buffet is incredible." Setting his plate carefully on his lap, he reached for the bottle of Pepsi out of his cooler. "The Pepsi here is good, but not like back home."

Wiping down the bottle with a napkin, he popped the cap off with a bottle opener attached to his keychain. I couldn't help but examine his every move. Everything about him suggested tact, an innate intelligence, power, and control. His movements were exact, his gaze acute, his pride in himself palpable. But as we ate, I noticed he seemed more anxious than usual. To relax him I asked, "So, how are things going with you?"

"Things are coming along. I'm looking forward to the work week being over. And I'm looking forward to going to the Caspian Sea for a day trip this weekend."

"That sounds like a fun time."

"Yeah, but there's more," he said. "I thought it would be nice if you came with me."

I couldn't help but laugh. "You mean you want to meet my father?"

"Sure, why not?"

"Really?" I said. "No, you don't mean that."

"Who do you think you're saying no to?"

Was this how he spoke to others at the job? And now wants to talk to me like this? Overwhelmed by a sudden surge of fear, I prayed someone else would enter the courtyard. Gently returning my food in its bag, I was prepared to leave. "Thanks for lunch, Curtis. I've got to get back to work now."

As I stood up to walk away, he begged, "No! Please forgive me! I'm sorry! There's been a lot of tension at work. I just thought you'd like the Caspian Sea is all."

Moved by his sincerity, I briefly paused. Yet, I was caught off guard by his sudden change. I examined him similar to how a witness would scrutinize suspects in a police lineup. Without the luxury of being separated by a glass wall, I was cautious in my next step.

"Please come back, let's finish talking." He pleaded. "Your friendship means so much. I'd hate to think that work stress would ruin it."

I returned to the bench. "I do like the Caspian Sea," I hesitated, "but I don't know *you* that well and things don't work like this with my family."

I was representative of the new Iranian woman, who had put education and traveling the world before settling down. I was aware my culture considered me too old for marriage. However, burying myself in work until the right man came along was all I had known. Dating meant dishonoring my family. "Just because we work together doesn't mean I *know* you. I'm sure you have a whole life in America separate from your life here."

Oh, how I prayed I was wrong.

"Okay." He smiled as if to indulge my interest. "I realize you haven't known me very long, Nusrat Rahimi. I'd hate for you to see me as just another know-it-all American."

He didn't give me a chance to respond before he asked, "What do you want to know?"

"Anything you think I should know."

"Well," he paused, "I'm recently divorced."

My heart sunk into my stomach. By now, I was sure my face looked like it fell flat.

"But that's all in the past. Please say you'll join me."

"We aren't married. I cannot go out with a man who is not my husband. As for what you've just shared, I'm surprised."

"Why?"

"You never speak of it. Certainly, it bothers you."

His brow furrowed. "Of course it was difficult, but the divorce is behind me now. You don't know how much you've helped me. Being so far from home can make a man lonely. To be friends with a beautiful woman makes me a lucky man."

What was it about him that wore away at my ideas of mixing with cultures? It wasn't intrigue. It was his sincerity in simple things, like the intensity by which his eyes glowed when he saw me smile. His constant flattery only strengthened my inner feelings. I couldn't explain the power he had over me. Finally, the charming gentleman I knew he truly was, appeared. "Tank you, Curtis. Perhaps it's the appropriate time you meet my parents?"

"It would be an honor."

All the while, my liberated heart whispered: *I want to be with you in a silent time, where nothing matters and the only things worth living for are the pauses of breath as we kiss like it was the kiss that you didn't see coming and it came, and you didn't move and I want to go with you anywhere, the Caspian Sea, the back of my father's Paykan, anywhere.*

"Great. I'll talk with them soon."

Later that evening, the servants brought furniture outside onto the veranda where I used to dream of being swept away as a child to a pink marble palace. I looked up at the sky as if asking it for guidance. I felt as though I was a simple woman who didn't need a man's love. My desire lived in the act of pouring my love into someone. In my mind swam the fact that I had never dreamt of marrying a man who saw me as brilliant, found my modesty alluring, and above all else, American. An intense pink appeared above the sun as it set over the mountainous skyline.

Could I imagine life away from home? Marveling at the endless beauty of the sky, it came to me. Now was the perfect time to marry and start a family. Soon the sky turned black. The house, the courtyard, and the fountain were lit by the stars. As I walked back inside, the sound of faraway thunder echoed in the air like a cracking belt. Expecting to see lightning, I turned and only saw the stillness of the night. I entered the living room and joined my parents for tea, a perfect time to bring up Curtis. Overtaken by joy, they immediately inquired as to when I would invite him to the house. But, I wasn't ready just yet. Coming to the house meant marriage would soon follow.

A week went by with thoughts of Curtis plaguing my mind. I knew the idea of premarital relations was sinful, but my daydreams were frequent and vivid. These thoughts left me feeling guilty but were so all-consuming that it became a nightly ritual for me to remove my night garments, close my eyes, lay back on the smooth, cotton sheets, and release my inhibitions. I just couldn't stop the visions of him kissing my lips. A never before desire I now had to dominate this strong figure came over me. I saw myself slowly removing all of my clothes. Delighting in him begging whether vocally or with the immediacy by which he would rip off his clothes, I wanted to feel his skin against my breast. *Oh Allah, forgive me!* Trying to stave off what I felt would complete me, I held my desires for Curtis at bay. Despite the fears my aunties had expressed about their wedding nights, I didn't shrink at the possibility of someday performing the deed that was expected by women. The idea of releasing all of my pinned up passion was exciting. I wanted to live out my fantasy of being safe in the arms of my naked husband. Trusting he would make an excellent first impression, by that May, I had invited him to my parent's house for dinner. While James continued to weigh me down with negativity about Curtis, I knew the job provided Curtis with the perfect social context in which to interact with my parents. I had discovered that he picked up on the power of eye contact, the customary importance of teatime, and how to correctly pronounce "hello" and "good-bye" in Farsi. I saw how Curtis set himself upon the task of learning something deeper about Iranian tradition and culture by trying to socialize with Iranian men at work. Sending his driver to take me home after work during the week and wherever I pleased to go on the weekend was a plus. Curtis wasn't the "arrogant American" I once imagined. Now, I saw him for who I knew he was all along, *my knight in shining armor.*

CHAPTER FOUR

The idea of being the topic of discussion between Nusrat and her parents over the past month gave Curtis hope this evening would come. He parked and looked up at the front door. Walking towards the home, the scent of early May roses lingered in the air. He saw Nusrat standing between her parents as if they were waiting to welcome him, the first American ever, into their home. Approaching them, Curtis reached out to shake her father's hand. "Assalam Alaikum, Mr. Rahimi." Curtis turned to greet Mrs. Rahimi. He hoped to conceal his shock at the striking resemblance between her and Nusrat. Mrs. Rahimi, still a youthful woman, appeared as if she participated in an unspoken fashion competition. Wearing a black sari with a purple velvet crocodile-print bust, she stood before Curtis like a queen, extending the top of her soft hand for him to kiss. "Nice to meet you, Mrs. Rahimi," he kissed her hand. "I see where Nusrat gets her beauty."

Curtis could have waited until he was invited into the house, but a strong sense of urgency led him to confront the current situation head-on. This impatience had served him oddly well throughout his life. It was also what encouraged him to jump into endeavors headfirst. He came to believe his calm, but confident bravado would win over his most ardent opposition. With that notion foremost in his mind, Curtis didn't wait to enter the front door and remove his shoes before broaching the purpose of his visit. Mrs. Rahimi had little time to retract her hand from the pre-greeting position before Curtis turned to Mr. Rahimi in one fluid motion. "I'm asking for your blessing to marry your daughter, sir."

Mr. Rahimi's eyebrows raised towards his thinning hairline conveyed his unexpected pleasure by Curtis' firm but serene demeanor. "Thank you for honoring our customs, young man," Mr. Rahimi firmly shook his hand, inviting Curtis into the home. They proceeded to walk down the main corridor on a sea of Persian rugs which meticulously covered the marble flooring up into the big hall. Mr. Rahimi patted him on the back and said, "Our daughter is quite fond of you and we welcome you with open arms."

Gleaming with satisfaction, Curtis approached a slim mahogany table with various pictures in wooden frames. He saw grey-bearded, unsmiling men with white turbans holding canes. He guessed the men were Ayatollahs, the elders Nusrat had told him about recently at work. Knowing the power and status behind this fact was not yet clear to him. Gazing at the pictures as if trying to make sense of them, Curtis' intrigue in his future bride heightened. Mr. Rahimi pointed to a picture. "This is Nusrat at age five. She had the rare opportunity to attend the first-ever kindergarten in Iran."

"Very nice."

Curtis' understanding of class was determined by race, black and white. Therefore, he couldn't quite grasp the prestige associated with Nusrat's religious family. He had not known that their faith-based affiliation gave them access to certain luxuries like the furniture in their house and discounted rates to travel back and forth to England. He saw something in one more picture that caught his eye: a bearded man who sat in a Rolls Royce in the midst of what appeared to be thousands of people.

"Mr. Rahimi that's a very nice car! What year is it?"

"Thank you, Curtis, I'm not sure of the year myself, but that's not my family's car. The king sent a driver to pick up my father to do Friday prayer." He pointed to the picture again. "That's my father on his way to the Arg mosque."

"And who are all those people in the street crowding the car?"

"Those are my father's followers walking to the mosque."

"Wow, that's incredible."

In awe of their beautiful home, everything so overwhelmingly elegant, Curtis believed Iranians had a love for exquisite things. As he continued walking with Mr. Rahimi, the silk curtains trimmed in intricate hand-beaded designs struck his eye. The equally ornate runners placed on the dining room table were inviting. On top of them stood two small mountains of fresh bananas, grapes, cucumbers, and oranges in lavish silver platters. Curtis had learned this was a staple of the Iranian home.

Finally, he noticed Mr. Rahimi motioned him to take a seat. The chair, a fancy high-back with golden silk fabric and careful stitching reminded him of a throne he once saw in a film. For the first time in his life, he felt regal. It was as if Curtis became the lead character in the black and white movies he had dreamt about as a child. Only now the dream was in Technicolor. It wasn't Errol Flynn or William Powell, but *his* name emblazoned across the marquee and underneath it the name of his exotic co-star, Nusrat Rahimi.

Curtis sat facing an equally elaborate English rolled arm sofa where Nusrat placed herself between her parents. With a deep sigh, he noticed how she crossed her legs in a way that revealed more than usual. At that moment, she was a sensual goddess who overwhelmed his libido with her femininity. He averted his eyes in an attempt to quell his urges while his mind raced with carnal longing. Mr. Rahimi's voice stole Curtis' attention. "Nusrat has learned how to cook in a way that you will find pleasing." Her father stated matter-of-factly, "You will be happy with her. However, I must warn you that she doesn't like watering plants and she has killed several New Year fish."

Not sure of how to respond appropriately, Curtis gave him a blank stare. After a long, uncertain silence, he finally replied, "I love her *anyway.*"

"Smart answer, Curtis," Mr. Rahimi said while holding his belly as if to keep himself from completely erupting, "but I was joking!"

⇌ ⇋

Later that evening, I saw my mother and Curtis sitting together as if they had known each other for years. Side by side, their backgrounds were different as night and day. The language barriers made it nearly impossible for anything beyond basic conversation to be understood. Yet they appeared identical in gesture letting their eyes lead the conversation. I wondered how long it was going to take Curtis to realize Maman didn't speak English. By the looks on their faces, it didn't matter. Maman smoked her cigarette and nodded intently in response to Curtis' engaging conversation. It almost made me laugh out loud, but like Maman, I was dazzled by his efforts to connect with us.

Once he left, my parents called everyone in the family to share the news. They cautiously put off telling my grandfathers and the other elders in the family. Sad but true, their traditional Islamic values wouldn't let them feel joy for Cain and I getting together. Though highly respected, my parents were considered progressives in their social circles and knew how to tread wisely with the elders. Unlike the aggressive, rude, and outspoken image Curtis projected at work, my parents cataloged him as a romantic American who put family first. But it was common wisdom, especially among the elders, that westerners were not to be trusted.

Maman and Baba told me that Curtis was as handsome as I was beautiful which is why they were taken aback with some of the reactions from the family about his proposal. Word spread fast and many of my cousins who considered themselves to be more glamorous and deserving of the prestige that came from marrying an American, whispered behind my back, "How could she get an American man?" "Is he going to marry someone like her, someone so plain, who doesn't even wear clothes from Paris?"

While my parents sensed jealousy and ill-will from some family members, the overall consensus was that everyone was happy I was finally doing it. Though they would decline their invitation, the elders' concern about "the American" were somewhat calmed when they learned he was covering all the wedding expenses.

That night I couldn't sleep. The vision of my wedding day took over. My mind raced one thousand miles per hour with questions: Who would make my dress? Who would I invite? Which Auntie would make the shireen pollo, wedding rice? When would I quit my job? Would my father be offended if I didn't want my wedding reception at the Iranian Oil Company Country Club?

My anxiety worsened until it was unbearable. I got up from my bed and felt the perspiration in my palms. I felt my body collapse and my legs gave way. Thinking to reach for the glass of water I had left on the nightstand, I instead found myself knees bent and head bowed on the prayer rug already laid out facing the direction of Mecca. The rug was a gift from my grandfather when I was five beginning to learn Arabic and study the Quran. In a moment of heightened awareness, I raised my eyes and stared helplessly at my reflection in the gold trimmed mirror that hung above the footstool in my room. So many times before I had prayed and asked Allah for guidance, but this time I felt a raw sense of desperation and fear of what to do next. *Oh Allah, please guide me.* I believed this episode was meaningful, a test of my resolve to fully step into the sanctity of matrimony. This was really happening.

⚔ ⚔

The last Thursday in May was hot, a perfect day to call in sick for a Caspian Sea escape. Driving two hours just to get a glimpse of the clear blue water and green mountains was a lovely idea for our first outing.

It was when Curtis parked on the side of the road that I noticed no other cars were there. The thought of having the beach all to ourselves was romantic. Excited about the possibilities of it all, I waited for him to open my door. We walked hand-in-hand to the beach. The sun, like a bursting mix of pomegranate and nectarine colors, gave life to the day. The fresh smell of water sliced through the air and the taste of sea salt danced on the tip of my tongue. I looked back to see how far we were from the car and saw only our footprints in the sand. If it weren't for my scarf, my hair would have waved like a flag against the breeze.

"When I was a child my parents came here. It was always crowded." I said as I scanned the horizon with more experienced eyes. I then turned looking intently at Curtis who was now unbuttoning his shirt.

"The water looks great! I can't wait to jump in."

"Jump in?" I knew my face said it all. "I thought we were going to enjoy the beach with a walk. I don't swim and I don't have a bathing suit."

We stood there listening to the gurgling sound of the water against the rocks as it withdrew itself back into the sea. This was more soothing than gazing upon the rocks and shells themselves. Then he stopped walking and faced me. "As you wish."

And for the first time, he kissed my hand, igniting an electric pulse that grew throughout my body. With the subtle crashing of the waves massaging my feet, I wanted more than ever to feel the brush of his lips touch mine. I looked both ways to make sure no one else was on the beach.

"I love you, Nusrat. Don't worry. Relax. No one will see."

As I watched him unfold the blanket, I felt a sense of ease. He placed it and the basket on the sand. Yes, I was completely alone with him. It was as if every muscle in my body relaxed pushing away any hint of nervousness. As we sat down, Curtis held my hand as a comforting guide. The firm grip of his hand enveloped the pillowy softness of my moist palm. My hand slid into his like that of a finely crafted glove. It was then that I felt the pulse of my heart beat in unison with his. Then I noticed him leaning forward with caution and restraint. There was a quality in his eyes, one that I had seen several times in the computer room that drew me to him. My eyes froze at the wonderment and anticipation of our lips touching. *Was this happening?* I blinked once. Then, our lips met leaving me to abandon any lingering fears in my mind. I leaned back upon the blanket, my acceptance quickly signaling submission. In no time I felt his body adjusting to the immediate circumstance. His weight upon me heightened all my senses. The smell of him, the taste of him, the sound of him breathing with the waves crashing in the background was all so perfect, exceeding my fantasy of the first kiss.

"I love you too Curtis," I said softly, "but we must wait until the wedding night."

My nipples must have budded through my dress as Curtis' eyes were drawn to my breasts. Afraid he couldn't contain his desires as I fought my own, I felt that I had to keep things under control so I reminded him, "I can't dishonor my family. I can't let this happen."

"We won't. Just let me do *this*."

Our lips met again and I gave way to the fire within.

Just before sunset, he took me home. That night I played the entire day over and over again in my mind and wondered if he believed me when I said, "Trust me, it will be worth the wait. We have to do this right. Our wedding night will be special."

CHAPTER FIVE

I quit my job in June and married Curtis on August 4, 1976. My family's reputation was a little tarnished by the elders' disapproval. But that didn't stop my parents from providing me, their only daughter, a memorable wedding. The three hundred and fifty guests danced and sang, and praised me on how beautiful I was as a bride. The men embraced Curtis, welcoming him into the family, while the single women wandered around. My parents, who radiated pride, had accepted the first American into the family. Saddened by the absence of the elders, I realized just how modern and liberal I was in contrast to their ancient beliefs that anything Western, including my husband, was evil.

I had a wedding sofreh fit for a queen, a gown designed by a reputable seamstress, and a five-tier cake instead of the traditional three-tiered. Local bakers made special provisions for my wedding, making it possible for me to share with my guests a sea of sweets only made during Norouz. When my mother asked Curtis if a one million toman mahr, a gift from the man to woman before the marriage was consummated, was too much, he gladly provided it. This was an unheard of amount as the average mahr was ten thousand toman which usually came in the form of jewelry, not cash. One million toman was enough money to purchase ten homes in a prime location if I wanted. I could claim this at any time during our marriage or if we were ever to divorce. Of course, I wished the best for our marriage, but I was comforted in knowing that if anything should happen, I would be financially covered. In return, Curtis' only request appeared reasonable: *if I got pregnant, he asked that the child be born in America.*

I didn't have a problem with his offer because it was an ideal reason for me to visit my husband's country.

During our wedding night, I tricked myself into believing Curtis was also making love for the first time when I had known otherwise. I wondered if my lovemaking was better than his first wife. I fought off the images, acknowledging something raw in the way he touched me, in the way he took his time. It prompted me, a virgin, to see his vulnerability.

Just weeks after the wedding, at the end of August, a fluctuation in temperature signaled the transition from summer to fall. I walked in on Baba looking to the distant mountains from the kitchen. Then, we heard the gardener reciting Rumi to an audience of leaves. Ironing his handkerchiefs, Baba chuckled and set them aside. "I'm just here thinking of your luck with finding a husband like Curtis."

"Thank you, Baba," I kissed him on the cheek. " It means so much."

I knew my parents felt contented about Curtis, a man who had fought a war and saved lives, a man who would tear up and pray for his fellow fallen soldiers out loud. When it came to me, he had complied with converting from Christianity to Islam and happily took on his Muslim name, Ali (though we rarely called him Ali, it was the name he signed on our wedding papers). My parents respected him, a man to whom money wasn't everything. Sparing no expense, Curtis had given me the wedding of my dreams. He wasn't just a fantasy, he was my ideal mate in the flesh.

"It was just yesterday he offered you a wedding ring in front of the family. And now, you're a woman right before my eyes."

But deep down I feared my life was too good to be true. My grandmother expressed her feelings of remorse for missing my wedding and convinced my grandfather to host a grand dinner in our honor. So happy with my grandfather's change of heart, I eagerly anticipated him showering us with prayers and well wishes. Hence, my disappointment from learning my husband still resented them for not showing up to the wedding initially. I thought this was an ideal opportunity for Curtis to meet my grandparents. One could only imagine my devastation when my entire family showed up except for my husband. My grandmother had spent all week with the help of my aunties in preparing the dinner. All the time and money they had put into cooking and decorating the hall had meant nothing to Curtis. It was rumored that he was at a bowling alley drinking beer with a co-worker. The embarrassment and shame he caused me angered my grandparents who seethed with a profound sense of disrespect. "Nusrat Joon, are you sure you want to make a life with this man?" My grandfather asked. "We can make arrangements for the marriage to disappear if it would suit you."

Publicly, I held Curtis' behavior to being homesick, but privately, I had known better. It was a rude and hurtful choice for him to skip the dinner. Not understanding the customs and culture just yet wasn't going to be an acceptable excuse. And still, for me, everything was about his charm and charisma which were both compelling and confusing. It was the perfect mix, I believed, for an exciting marital love affair. So when he gave the excuse, "I was at work tying up loose ends on a big project," I buried the pain and chose to meet him with forgiveness instead of bitter resentment.

We stayed with my parents for two months after our marriage. I maintained the household in a fashion I thought would both satisfy my parents and husband. I cooked, cleaned, washed clothes, and continually sought ways to please Curtis. He reciprocated by showering me with compliments and hints of his happiness ranging from "Oh Nusrat, this dinner is delicious!" to "How did I get so lucky to have such a beautiful wife?" or my favorite, "Come here, I want to kiss my wife."

He knew just what to say to put a smile on my face.

⇒ ⇐

One day in October, the air was surprisingly thick and intolerable as I walked home from the market with the ingredients for the night's meal. Although I was used to the heat, something made me unusually nauseous. The feeling had consistently gotten worse. Reaching home I took a break to fan myself, but I was overwhelmed and lost consciousness.

A short time later, I awoke to see my mother dipping a towel in a pan and wringing out the excess water. The feeling of the cool cloth placed gently on my forehead was refreshing.

"Relax, Nusrat Joon," my mother said as she repeated the regimen. "The doctor just left. Don't worry, all is well."

"What happened? How did I get here?"

"I found you by the door with the items from the market. The heat was too much for you…in your condition."

"My condition?"

"You've been blessed with a gift from Allah. You are with child," my mother said, her lips curled at the corners into a loving smile.

I had heard of this happening, but I didn't think I would become a mother so soon after my wedding night. I barely felt secure in being a wife. Now, Allah saw it fit to bless me with a *baby*? I remembered the subtle voices of my mother's friends as they gathered to enjoy each other's company and share the latest gossip. I envisioned the group of covered middle-aged women in the kitchen preparing meals as the eldest spoke of the blessings that came with conceiving early for the glory of a husband. Perhaps this was the blessing we needed to warm up to the elders? I couldn't wait until Curtis returned home to share the news. But, what was I to make of a sneaking feeling that crept into my mind and left me a bit anxious? Whispering a prayer of thanks, I drifted off to sleep. A few hours later I awoke and saw Curtis had fallen asleep in a chair by my bedside. Smelling the faint fragrance of red tulips in a vase on the table next to my bed brought a sudden calm to my weary body. Within minutes, I returned to dreaming of America.

Like many other Iranians my age, I dreamed of visiting the West. Curtis' words, "You'll love my country," only stirred my excitement more. I had fallen more deeply in love with him and the possibility of going there. I fantasized about what it would be like to visit: I would take a picture standing right in front of the White House in a fur coat and black sling-back heels. I would be the envy of my aunties and cousins. Maybe I would be lucky and catch a glimpse of President Carter sitting by a window in clear view. I imagined him waving at me and smiling. I saw myself filled with excitement at the thought of returning home and telling all of my American experience. Yes, I could see it: my family traveling from near and far just to hear about my time in the USA. We would be gathered in tea and sweets as I passed around my photos basking in the attention.

A lump of fat, a fresh embodiment within one camel hump. Gone are the days the milkman leaves glass bottles at the door. An Aries sun sets beauty that only the blind can see. I know you're doing your best carrying me. I know all this traveling isn't easy. I hear your cries. I smell the fire. I will come on the new moon.

CHAPTER SIX

On December 22, 1976, I arrived in America for the *first* time to give birth to my *first* child. Walking through the airport and all the way until we caught a cab, strangers wished Curtis and I a "Merry Christmas" or "Happy Holidays!" Unlike Curtis who seemed unfazed by the merriment, I was moved by the sweet reception from total strangers receiving me into their country. For years I had heard of the great lengths Americans went through to celebrate Christmas and was eager to experience it for the first time.

The sky was overcast and it was cold. My husband helped me into the car before loading the luggage into the trunk. I greeted the cab driver, then took a seat. I noticed he turned up the heat and put his leather gloves on before he helped Curtis with the luggage. Once we got on the road, the cab driver fumbled with the radio tuner to get the red line on a clear signal until he found a clear connection on a news station. The voice on the radio announced snow in the forecast, but no flurries had fallen yet. Curtis, who seemed unusually quiet, informed me that his mother, a widow of only two years, had a hard time adjusting to life alone.

"My mother will be happy to have some company seeing that my big sister is tied up with her own family in New York for the holidays," he said.

He told me that it would take an hour to drive from Dulles airport to his mother's home in Takoma Park. Looking at my watch, I realized an hour had passed. I asked him, "How far are we?"

"We're almost there, this is the neighborhood I grew up in."

Paying extra attention to my surroundings as if to visualize my husband's past, I noticed an empty corner store, holly wreaths on front porches, and a middle-aged woman pushing a child in a stroller up the hill. I noticed the woman's brown skin was a stark contrast to the white scarf on her head and I was in awe of her beauty. Besides the cab driver, this was the first time I saw a black person up close. My first impression of America was that it was a place where cultural differences didn't get in the way of people living in the same communities. Of course, I was taught otherwise in school and heard of the sensitive race relations on the news. But there were no visible signs that Curtis ever grew up in a segregated neighborhood. The wide trees, steep hills and narrow streets at odd angles made Takoma Park, Maryland feel almost magical.

I remembered him telling me that his parents, Louis and Meredith Brown, moved in 1934, during the Great Depression. And how they had packed up his sister, Nunny, and left Nebraska for his father's new job as a government electrical engineer. Back then, Curtis said the area had bloomed with character that went well with a distinct small-town feel. At the same time, it bordered the nation's capital where one didn't know every neighbor's name. A perfect place to raise children, Curtis told me, where mothers prepared spaghetti dinners for Boy Scout fundraising, where families anticipated the Fourth of July parade, and it was safe to drink from the local springs. While I didn't know what it meant to skip rocks or catch tadpoles, Curtis mentioned he had done these things as a child at the Sligo Creek. There was also a rumor that President Harding's sister once lived down the street from his home. All this I had pieced together from Curtis' tales.

When we pulled up to the driveway, I was impressed by the large size of the house with its grand porch. I wondered why it was the only house on the street without a wreath. In the yard which was on the side of the house instead of the front, I saw an old car. It was hard for me to believe his mother would be driving a car like that or even driving at all. I didn't say anything about my initial scan of the surroundings, but I noted it all as if at once.

"Go ahead in the house." Curtis reached for his wallet in his back pocket to pay the cab fare. "I'll take care of our things."

The cab driver got out of the car to open the door for me. I wasn't able to button my coat all the way so I covered myself with a scarf hoping it would suffice. Once I stepped out the cab, a large wind of cold air blew my coat backward; it exposed my slightly budding stomach to the chill. Praying the cab driver didn't see, I immediately put the scarf on again and headed towards the stone driveway. At ten in the morning, I assumed Mrs. Brown would be awake anticipating our arrival. I looked forward to getting into the warm home. As I walked, I made sure not to trip on the uneven sidewalk leading to the side glass door. I remembered my father's last words to me before I left the airport in Iran: *Love always wins. Have an open heart and an open mind and don't forget to give your mother-in-law the piece of pure silver from us.*

I looked for a place to knock and then saw the doorbell button near the handle. I pressed it while looking through the glass door into the house. I saw a wooden table with one chair facing the window that had a clear view of the street. Four aloe plants were arranged on the table in mismatched plant vases. By the looks of the high stack of magazines next to a chair, I gathered it was a place she sat quite often. I couldn't make out what kind they were, but if I had to guess based off the food images, I would say they were cooking magazines. I thought it was odd for this area to be an entrance. I pressed the button again.

"I'm coming!" A frail yet authoritative voice called.

Within a minute, I saw her coming towards the door. Mrs. Brown looked to be in her eighties, but at the age of sixty-five, she was alive with energy even with a walker. Her thin white hair was short, I would say it looked manly. I was surprised to see her dressed in a flower-covered housecoat instead of something more formal like a dress. I wondered if she was sick. And still, I couldn't believe I was finally meeting the mother of my husband. Mrs. Brown humped over her walker taking one step at a time, "I'm coming!"

Giddy with excitement, I adjusted myself, making sure my coat sat nice and that a smile warmed my face. I then saw Mrs. Brown struggle to take a few more steps to open the door. I felt sorry for her and wished I could help her somehow. Finally, she approached the door.

"So you're Nusrat?"

Mrs. Brown's marble blue eyes cut at my face, then examined my belly. She knew we were expecting our first child.

"I see. My son brought you all the way here from *I-ran* huh?" She frowned. "How far along are you now?"

"I'm almost five months," I said in disbelief. Then, I gently leaned forward initiating a hug and immediately noticed her shoulders slightly raised. It was as if they were almost leaning back away from my embrace and her feet had paced backward. Flooded with regret, I wished I could transport myself home again with my family. Why was she so cold? Was she going to hug me? Kiss me or do something to show that she was happy to finally meet me? I wasn't accustomed to this type of welcome upon meeting someone regarded as family for the first time. The shock of the situation was too much. I was dumbfounded and confused. Was this an American ritual to gauge the heart of a person? Was this like how the rigid parents back home would react to a suitor as a test of worthiness for their daughter? For a minute my mind escaped to an alternate scene where his mother would say, "Of course you're five months! Come here and hug me Nusrat, my new daughter!"

But his mother, I instantly learned, was not one who hid her true feelings. She was certainly not going to hug me with a ten-foot pole. I looked to my husband for reassurance, for some sign that his mother's response was intended to mask her admiration. But, it didn't come and my heart was filled with resentment. He didn't see to it that his mother accepted me with similar affections that my family had showered him with back home. For the love of Allah, I was carrying his child.

"It's nice to finally meet you, Mrs. Brown."

Discouraged by her greeting, I couldn't understand why she wouldn't receive me with open arms. This would've been where I handed her the silver bracelet, a family heirloom, but I couldn't bring myself to do it. Did I come all the way here for this? I would have usually questioned, but processing, evaluating, and analyzing his mother overwhelmed me and nearly made me faint.

"Where's my son?" His mother looked out the door. I imagined she saw him taking out the luggage from the trunk.

"He's coming." My teeth chattered from the extended time in the cold. "He's bringing our luggage."

"I see." Mrs. Brown positioned herself more upright.

Couldn't she sense I wanted to get out of the cold? Where was her proper etiquette? Curtis appeared at the door. "Hi ma," he said without stopping to hug her or show any form of affection.

"Let me close this door before the cold gets in." Mrs. Brown said as my husband carried our luggage inside.

No smile, no formal introduction - nothing. It was as if he went down the street for cigarettes instead of returning from another country. And where was the Christmas spirit? Completely blown away, I wondered what type of family I had married into.

"Curtis!" His mother raised her voice as if fighting to finally get his attention. "Curtis, do you hear me calling you?"

She adjusted her walker to turn around then told me to follow her in. The smell of old urine odor hardly covered up by powder or perfume had hit my nose. It was clear that she was immune to her own scent. Curtis, who did not acknowledge it, must have been all too familiar with his mother's hygiene. She had made no attempt to make a decent first impression with even the simple ritual of bathing. In disbelief, I stepped carefully about the furniture filled apartment. In the living room were the first images that stood out to me: a table stacked with dishes designed in blue and white of a country farm, a spinning wheel coated in layers of dust, a davenport, an old pine chest filled with wooden blocks, three glass-topped end tables, a fireplace, and Mrs. Brown's recliner which faced the television. The house wasn't the mansion I anticipated and far from any of the comforts of home I had expected. It was more like a hoarder's paradise piled with antiques, some broken and others visually beyond repair. I feared that I would accidentally bump against something. I placed my hand over my womb and grew horrified at the thought of being pregnant for four months in such a place. Why would his mother keep all these things? And then my elbow bumped into a Mason jar which sat on a shelf next to me. It shattered on the floor leaving small pieces of electrical wiring and screws everywhere. I got down and managed as best as I could to pick it all up. "I'm so sorry Mrs. Brown."

"Those were just memories of my husband is all. Thank heaven he isn't here to see all of this. Shoot, he's probably rolling around in his grave."

I couldn't understand the significance of my small mistake or why it would infuriate a dead man. "Is everything okay Mrs. Brown?"

"When we first moved here, Louis took care of the plumbing, electrical, and minor carpentry repairs. I did the bookkeeping. All our renters paid on the first of the month. After saving for eight months, my husband purchased a new Chevy Fleetmaster. Nine years later, Curtis was born in the back seat. I think it was 1943. Yup, he came right out on Flower Avenue."

I was still waiting to hear a sound response. I couldn't understand the relationship between what she was saying and the mason jars. Mrs. Brown continued talking. "From the time we purchased the property in 1934 through the 1960's, we rented to young adults starting their lives. We never had a problem keeping our apartments occupied with clean and decent people. But things changed in the early '70s. Now, *you're* here. My husband's memories are all shattered."

What was that supposed to mean? Thankfully Curtis entered the room. I hoped he would distract our uncomfortable conversation.

"What is it ma?" I heard him say. "Don't you see that I'm trying to get us settled in?"

I took my coat off and had a seat, a move that didn't go unnoticed by his mother.

"I didn't say you could have a seat."

"Come on ma, we've been traveling for almost two days. Relax will ya!"

"Well..." Mrs. Brown looked at her son and then glared at me. "I just don't understand." The tension in her voice rose and instantly I feared something vile was to come next.

"How could you go to the other side of the world and bring this nigger to my home?"

What? I didn't know which was more alarming, the fact that he didn't live in a mansion or that his mother believed I was too stupid to understand what she had just said. She thought I was colored? I translated it into being a deplorable thing. How could a person dislike me for no reason? Who was she to tell me what I was or wasn't? What did Curtis tell her about me? My family? My country?

Oh, how I fought off the impulse to cry. Mrs. Brown's passion was so tragic that I was at a loss for words. How could my husband put me, his pregnant wife, in such a situation? I couldn't believe that I had agreed to give birth in America. Was this really happening? I had left my country, my family, and my job to be treated like *this*?

＝⫟ ⫟＝

Curtis carried my luggage into his bedroom now riddled with stacks of boxes, a mid-century four-dresser drawer, nightstand, and a thin, noisy mattress. His father's clothes hung in the closet that his mother more than likely couldn't bring herself to donate. I sat on the bed staring at my suitcase with no desire to unpack.

He stayed with me for three weeks before returning to his job and my family's home in Iran. Seeing to it that I had the best medical care, my husband found me an obstetrician, pediatrician for the baby, a doctor for my thyroid condition and stocked the pantry with rice, canned vegetables, and juice. He left a grocery list with his mother of foods for me to eat. By the time he left in February, I had entered my third trimester. The reality of being stuck with his mother was beyond depressing. I sobbed when Curtis left for the airport. His last words as he got into the cab were, "I love you. I promise this time will go by fast. Before you know it, we will be together as a family." He drew my chin towards his face, "You know I have to make money in Iran so that I can take care of you and the baby right?"

Wiping my tears from both eyes, I nodded and kissed him good-bye. Next, Curtis said parting words to his mother, "Please take care of my wife."

The latter of his farewell made me cringe. He had to know his mother was going to make this unbearable.

I saw promising my husband an American child was by far the biggest mistake I had ever made in my life. Back home I had no idea of what it meant to fulfill or endure having his child. Now, I was stuck. I didn't know it meant relying on his mother for an allowance to eat and taking the bus to the doctor's office. I didn't know his mother was going to make me eat bacon, a forbidden meat for Muslims to eat. I didn't know the highlight of my days was going to be dropping letters in the mailbox for Curtis and desperately waiting for his response. I didn't know his mother was going to refer to me as "colored" instead of my actual name. I didn't know that I would be perceived as ignorant to her racial discrimination against my family. I didn't know that I was going to be hated for the first time in my life. It was just February. I was about three and a half months away from my due date. *Wherever Allah was, I needed Him.*

I spent many of my waking hours in bed praying with my prayer beads, over my fate. I looked at the few pictures of my parents that I had kept in my wallet and it only made me weep more at the current state of my life. It was during these times where I would hear a strange thumping sound coming from the outside of my bedroom door. It was disturbing, but I surmised it was a mouse hitting the wall or the house settling. Next to my bedroom door was a skinny door that led to what Curtis once referred to as the "dungeon."

I remembered him telling me it was his father's hide-away from his mother. Curtis said it was his father's "sanctuary," the only place her wide hips couldn't squeeze through. A place, he concluded, where his mother had ultimately found a way to nag, nitpick, and drive his father "up a wall." Curtis' impersonation of his mother initially made me laugh. In a crow-like voice, he'd say, "Did you *mow* the lawn yet? Did you *fix* the leak in apartment four? Did you *remember* to give your boss my canned beets?"

It wasn't what he said that made me laugh, but the way he altered his voice to sound like a woman. Another funny thing was when he joked about how his father threatened his mother with Bible in hand, "If you don't shut up I swear to God I'll kill you woman!"

But when he told me how he found his father dead in the "dungeon" with the Bible held to his chest, I imagined his mother had pushed the poor man over the edge. Now, I was certain she led her husband to premature death.

After Curtis left, if I didn't have a doctor's appointment, I stayed at home sleeping or dreading to wake up to Mrs. Brown. I couldn't let her push me too far. I had to keep myself together for the sake of the baby. When *Wheel of Fortune* came on, I knew I could get some peace. Occasionally, in the late evenings, she threatened me with "You can't take the baby to Iran. If you do, you'll see what I'll do!"

I'd fall silent, infuriating her, and then I'd return to my room to watch Johnny Carson. One of these times, her anger got the best of her, and she followed me into my room yelling.

"Do you know who my father was? Did Curtis ever tell you? His name was Barak Livingston, the last Civil War veteran to die in Nebraska. I bet you didn't know that did you?

"No, Mrs. Brown, I didn't know that."

"Well, it's important for you to know. My father proudly served in the Union Army. Soon after the war, he started his family. He was a hard-working farmer who spent most of his days working the fields. My father taught us the importance of having a clean family tree and look at us now."

I didn't say anything. I merely let her speak to hear herself talk. Then she left my room to call her only friend, Diane. Beyond the sounds of the television and the creaks from the renters walking above, I heard her talking about me. She didn't have the decency to lower her voice or speak behind my back. I believed she wanted me to hear her say, "Bringing a damn foreigner into my house! Can you believe it, Diane? Can *you*?"

If it weren't that, she'd talk about "Curtis' betrayal to his race." Even if I snapped back, I figured it would upset my husband. But in reality, he wouldn't care. Who was I kidding? Look at the way he treated his mother. All I wanted to do was give birth and go back home.

Spending most of her days in the Lazy Boy recliner, his mother hardly cooked. She also preferred to sleep in the chair instead of in her bedroom. I thought it was because she missed her husband, but I was wrong. She slept there because it was the easiest way for her to prop her legs up to help with circulation as she faced the TV. When she wasn't glued to the screen, she delighted in the conveniences of frozen dinners like Stouffer's cream chipped beef and lasagna. But when she did cook, she prepared everything with either ham or bacon. My only choice was to eat around it or eat nothing at all. She didn't give a damn about my religion.

When I had to eat something despite her attempts at starving me, I'd make a meal out of putting chips and mayo between two slices of bread. She would sit in front of me and laugh as I ate. I knew what she was doing and saved my anger for when Curtis called. I told him, "You know your mother's kitchen is tiny! Imagine my big body and my pregnant belly in the kitchen! We don't fit. Every time I go to cook something she reminds me that it's *her kitchen*. What am I supposed to do? I have to eat, I'm pregnant *remember*? I clean the kitchen, but nothing is ever good enough for her. I don't want to be here. I've never felt like this my entire life."

His only reply was to remind me of how much more time I had before giving birth, "Only two more months to go."

Johnny Carson and Ali made this time bearable.

One Tuesday morning, I got off the bus and walked to the gynecologist's office. Walking through the glass door entrance, I saw Ali at his security desk and looked away in fear of our eyes meeting. I found a focal point on the wall: a poster advertising a new medicine. I acted like I was intently reading so as not to appear that I noticed him looking my way. Then I nonchalantly walked towards him to get to my appointment.

"Good morning Sister. How are the *two* of you doing?"

Oh my, he noticed my growing stomach. "Thank you, Mr. Ali. We are fine. How are you and your family?"

"My mother and father," he said in a way that I took wishing "family" meant a wife and children, "I miss them dearly, but you know how it is." He opened the second set of double doors that led to the doctor's office. "Ma Salama."

His last words gave me goose bumps. Was it the familiarity of his accent that made me tingle? I wanted to thank him for treating me like a human being. Instead, I smiled and said, "Shukran Ali, have a nice day."

These brief, but special, encounters gave me the boost I needed to get through my days. Having the baby was always on my mind. Traveling back home would soon be my reality. I couldn't wait to forget this trip ever happened.

Finally, after living with his crazy mother for three months, there was a break from the constant tension. I couldn't believe it. She let me cook kibbeh, ground lamb with bulgar wheat. For the first time, we sat and enjoyed a meal together.

"What's this Nusrat?" She asked me in between bites. "It's delicious! And look at how pretty you look today."

"Thank you, Mrs. Brown, but I don't think I look any different today than I did any other day. If anything, I'm larger than a cow."

"Of course you look pretty. Let me tell you something. When Louis and I got engaged, Charles Lindbergh (before he was famous) gave us a plane ride. Lindbergh winked at me as he helped me into the cockpit. Louis didn't notice, but for me, fireworks exploded. It was as if I was Ms. America. I'll never forget that moment. That's what happens when you get older. You have your memories to hold you together."

For a brief moment, it appeared as if Mrs. Brown had a real smile on her face. It didn't take long for me to expect something negative to follow.

"What a nice story Mrs. Brown. This is Kibbeh, I make it back home all the time," I said, "I'm glad you like it."

"I do. It's very tasty." She took a bite and chewed as if examining the ingredients in her mind. "You look surprised." She made a Grinch-like smile. "*Oh*, you *think* I can't enjoy this?"

"It's not that. I'm just glad we can enjoy a moment together Mrs. Brown. That's all."

"It reminds me of the salmon cakes I used to make for Curtis when he was a boy. He loved my cooking you know. He used to jump in his seat and dig in! He still does. He loves it when I make my tuna fish casserole. That son of mine." She paused as if to recollect a thought from her mental Rolodex. "He sure was a joy and creative with his hands. Did he ever tell you about the wooden blocks his father made just for him? They're sitting in the green chest in the living room as we speak."

I couldn't believe the power my cooking had over Mrs. Brown. I mean the transformation was so drastic, almost like she was another person. She went on and on with memories of Curtis' childhood, which, of course, reflected her high opinion of her abilities as a caretaker and a homemaker. I was most surprised when she spoke of him on the bus leaving for the military.

"Curtis dropped out of high school and was immediately sent to Vietnam. My boy was forever changed. I'll never forget his last letters during the war when he ended his writing with "signed in blood."

"The way I see it is like this Nusrat." Mrs. Brown patted her mouth with a paper napkin. "They're good angels and they're bad angels." She took a sip of water from her paper cup and continued sharing her life's wisdom. "And, nobody has to be a good angel all the time. That's why I named my son Curtis. He was my well-mannered and naughty little angel. You know if you have a son, his name will be Curtis Brown Junior?"

Did she just tell me what our son was going to be named? "I see Mrs. Brown," I said before I got up and gathered the paper plates to throw in the trashcan. I wiped the table down. "I'm going to lay down now. I feel the baby moving a lot.

"Tell me something, has he written lately?"

"Yes, I got a letter from him yesterday. He's fine, just excited about the baby coming."

⊷⊶

Mrs. Brown wasn't all bad. I bet she secretly liked the idea of a baby being around the house but didn't want to admit it.

"Before you go to bed, let me tell you this."

She grabbed for my hand.

"My children had to stop going to Glen Echo. The coloreds took over and ruined everything. Don't you get it? Me and my husband, when he was alive, worked hard, paid taxes, paid all our bills on time. We didn't bother anybody. We didn't want any trouble. We should have been able to live our lives without seeing the coloreds is all."

"Okay Mrs. Brown, I have to lay down now." I rubbed my belly. "The baby is making me tired."

"How far along are you anyway?"

"I just started my ninth month."

"You know you're *not* taking the baby to Iran. *Right?*"

"Yes, Mrs. Brown. Yes, I know."

CHAPTER SEVEN

It was March of 1977 and my ninth month of pregnancy was upon us. My parents had every right to see their first-born grandchild. If necessary, I knew they would pay for a return ticket for the baby and me. This fact gave me comfort in my current situation. I dozed off to bed with the echo of his mother's voice, now a familiar sound, and tried to ignore her phone conversation: "She cooks and uses my kitchen. Diane, you know I don't like Nusrat in my kitchen. It just drives me nuts!"

It was just a matter of time when Mrs. Brown's negativity was going to be out of my life. Then four weeks later, in mid-April, her sister Dorothy and her husband visited. They drove from Nebraska to install a new kitchen floor in Mrs. Brown's apartment. I just knew my mother-in-law now had two more people she could vent to about me and my pregnancy. But to my surprise, I would be proven wrong.

Their plans changed when my water broke at four o'clock in the morning. When I woke up out of my bed and stood up, the water trickled down my leg without me having any control. I wanted to believe it was happening due to the baby pushing on my bladder. But, when I went to the living room to let Mrs. Brown know, the water didn't stop dripping.

"Mrs. Brown," I whispered. "Mrs. Brown, I think my water broke."

Fearing the moment I had been waiting on was finally here, I ran to the kitchen and called Curtis, "I think it's time!"

I resented him for not being by my side, but with the water creeping down my legs I started to panic. "What am I supposed to do? You're all the way over there and I'm all the way over here!"

"Go wake mom up."

"You think she's going to *help* me? Do you know *your* mother?" I said before I hung up the phone.

Returning to the living room, I saw her in a deep sleep with her mouth wide open. Once I tapped her on the shoulder, her eyes opened. She looked at me as if she was up, not startled. She finally spoke, "Ok. I'm coming."

I wondered what I did in my current life or past life for God to punish me with such luck. At a loss for words, I had no time for this and went for the telephone.

Just as I was about to dial 911, Dorothy walked in the kitchen, "What's going on Nusrat?" She wrapped her robe around her waist, "Are you okay?"

"I think my water broke. What do I do?"

"Is it coming out without your control?"

"Yes!"

"Well, my dear, it sounds like we're about to have us a baby!"

"But, Mrs. Brown won't wake up."

"Don't you worry your pretty head. I'm going to take you to the hospital. I'm going to tell everyone that the baby is my grandchild. Get your bag and let's go."

"But I have to clean this mess."

"Do you want to have the baby *here*? Don't worry about that, my husband will get it."

Dorothy lined three plastic trash bags in the front seat for me. "There you go, my dear. You know the hospital is right up the street so hold on alright?" Instead of pulling forward out of the driveway, Dorothy backed into Mrs. Brown's car. "Jesus Christ!" She got out the car to assess the damage. "Just a bump. Nothing serious. I won't tell if you don't."

"I'm not saying a word."

Feeling one of the bags on the back of my thigh, I looked out the car's window and prayed I didn't ruin Dorothy's car seat. I had wished I was in Iran with Curtis by my side. But the sights of Takoma Park's garden apartments reminded me that I was far removed from home and my husband. Staring at the rooftops as the dew glistened the grass, my eyes shifted to my face. I looked past my image in the right side mirror to a red painted fire hydrant. Meanwhile, Dorothy looked back and forth between the road and me as I prayed to get to the hospital in time.

"Well, it doesn't look like history will be repeating itself here today."

"What do you mean?"

"Curtis was delivered right there." She pointed to the fire hydrant underneath the Flower Avenue sign.

For a second, I imagined what it would be like to have a similar fate and then I remembered what my mother had said, "Be strong, once you have the baby, we will see you soon. Hold on." I closed my eyes to focus on breathing.

Dorothy parked in front of the hospital and reminded me, "I'm sure the women in your family gave birth at home like the women in our family did. But you my dear are about to make history giving birth to a baby in an American hospital!"

The unknown was scary, lonely, and unnerving. Dorothy may have seen it all over my face as she took my hand in hers and said, "Don't worry. I won't leave you. Not for a minute."

We made it to the hospital just in time to learn I only dilated one centimeter. As promised, Dorothy was by my side the entire day. Thirteen hours later, at 5:00 p.m., the doctor determined the baby was breech and a c-section was required. Dorothy called Mrs. Brown to give her the news, but she didn't answer the phone.

Just as I was about to panic, I heard a familiar sound. The intermittent clicking and jolting of a walker came to my ear and then Mrs. Brown walked through the door. She was her usual hostile and commotion-stirring self.

"Why did you leave a mess all over my home, Nusrat?" She made her way to a chair by the window. "I've spent all day on my knees cleaning up after you. You know I've got a bad back!"

I noticed Dorothy growing irritated by the way she watched her sister carry on with me. Her eyes rolled in the same way mine did whenever Mrs. Brown got on my nerves. Dorothy finally said, "You might as well have shouted louder drawing more attention to the room Meredith,"

But Mrs. Brown just ignored her sister and continued, "I would've been here sooner, but I had to wait for the neighbor to fix my flat tire."

Although raised in the same home as Mrs. Brown, Dorothy was inclined to defend me from her sister's evil. I'm so thankful God answered my prayer by sending her to help me.

"It's five o'clock, Meredith." Dorothy leaned towards Mrs. Brown. "Where have you been all this time? It's just like you to be this way." She made direct eye contact with her sister. "It reminds me of when you weren't even there when Nunny had her first child. What's wrong with you? Didn't you learn your lesson from how much you hurt your own daughter? Why would you want to do that to Nusrat when Curtis can't even be here? What's *wrong* with you?"

Mrs. Brown looked behind her back as if to see if there was anyone else in the room Dorothy could've been speaking to at that moment. I knew it was about to get ugly.

"Hold your horses, Dorothy. I'm the one who's been home all day cleaning up her mess."

Mrs. Brown pointed at me.

"It's not my fault I had a flat. What did you want me to do? Walk? Fly? I did my best. Now, I'm here. *Right?*"

"I hear what you're saying Meredith, but it's simply unacceptable."

"Are you with me or against me Dorothy?"

At that moment, I wondered if it had hit Mrs. Brown the baby was coming. And what kind of mother wouldn't want to help her daughter during labor? What was it going to take for her to accept *I* was having her grandchild? In my position, there was nothing for me to do but cry.

"I would cry too if I left that mess for someone else to clean."

"Just shut up why don't you?" Dorothy said. "My husband cleaned it up, he's still over there getting things straight. It's no bother to you, so stop."

For two straight hours, Mrs. Brown obsessed over the wet floor and the baby going to Iran. I saw the concerned faces of the nurse and doctor and how they looked as if they feared to interfere in family affairs. I believed there was more than a flat tire that prevented her from coming sooner. What about her true feelings about the baby to be born? I could bet she believed coming earlier would've made her look too eager to welcome a baby who she believed was supposedly "ruining her family tree." I knew better though. Underneath it all, she was happy. Before they took me for surgery, the doctor asked, "Do you want me to ask your mother-in-law to leave?"

"No Doctor," I said, "that's just the way she is."

The moment I had been waiting for was finally here. Dorothy kissed me on the cheek and offered a few comforting words. Anything other than a successful outcome wasn't possible, this was going to be smooth and great. I was put to sleep and didn't become alert until I was in recovery.

When I finally awoke from surgery, I saw the nurses, but I didn't see Mrs. Brown, Dorothy, or the baby. And then I panicked like a crazy woman.

"Where's my baby? Is the baby healthy? Where's *my baby*! Answer *me*!"

A nurse finally embraced my arm and spoke calmly, "Your baby girl is just fine." She pulled out my chart and read, "She was born at 7:30 p.m. on April 18, 1977, via c-section. The baby was born with jaundice and has twelve toes, *six* on each foot."

An instant peace fell upon my soul. "A *girl*? A *girl...*" I repeated to convince myself it was real, "A little girl."

⇒⊹ ⊹⇐

Four days passed after the c-section before I could open my eyes wide and make decisions, not yet able to walk. Mrs. Brown told me that it rained all morning. The sun made a grand entrance by noon, a sight I hadn't seen from my dark hospital room with the shades closed. Besides a little jaundice, I knew my baby was healthy and that's all that mattered. Learning my baby girl was born with twelve toes was a fact that did *not* disrupt my enjoyment. I stared at her round peach face and melted at the sight of the tiny white bow in her hair. "A love like no other" is how I felt described my feelings. It was completely different than what I ever felt for my husband. Then I remembered how I wished he was by my side.

Staring at the hospital television screen, I saw a commercial where a father was in a nursery visiting his baby. I visualized Curtis' excitement at seeing his daughter in the nursery like that. Thoughts circled in my mind. I recreated my daughter's birth where my husband encouraged me that I could do it, wiped my forehead with a damp cloth, greeted me with an extravagant bouquet and whispered in my ear, "I love you and thank you."

Of course, it was more romantic than what really happened. To be honest, it wasn't like I remembered most of it anyway. Then I heard Mrs. Brown stirring in her seat and shoved all my desires for Curtis away. She sat next to me in a chair crocheting a blanket concentrating on her pattern. She spoke as if her silence was bringing her pain. "Tell me the truth Nusrat, what do you plan on doing with my grandbaby?"

At first, I was about to argue but chose not to, it would've taken too much energy, the energy I needed to take care of myself and the baby. "Mrs. Brown, you know we've planned to return to Iran. My family wants to see Yvonne too."

"Yvonne? Darling, her name is *Nicole* Nardin Brown. We named her after my mother and let you have the middle name."

I assumed "we" meant Mrs. Brown and Dorothy, *not* Mrs. Brown and my husband. Where was Dorothy? I wanted to plead with her to change the name, but I knew it was hopeless. I had to view my life like this to survive, I had to remind myself that I was only there temporarily. My baby was born which meant Curtis would return soon. It wouldn't be long before we started our life in Iran, far away from his mother.

"We're taking the baby to Iran."

"What about my son? He's worked so hard to provide for you and the baby. Don't you think he has the right to come back home and raise his child in America?

"I promised to give him an American child. Living here was *never* the plan. It was always understood we would return to my home."

"How dare you! So ungrateful."

"Ungrateful for what? Having a baby here and dealing with you? I can't wait to get home. I did my part and now we'll be on our way. Enjoy the time you have with the baby because it *won't* last long."

Two weeks after I left the hospital, I sat on an Amtrak train headed for Baltimore to the Vital Statistics Administration building. With just three dollars, my baby, and a grey cobra skin pocketbook that my mother purchased in Bombay, I was determined to change her name. On my return trip back to Takoma Park, I hugged and kissed Yvonne Nardin Brown, a newborn that had another name visibly crossed out on her birth certificate. It didn't matter anymore because her toes became the new issue and more cause for arguing than anything else. They weren't a forbidden subject, it's just that Mrs. Brown believed the baby was mentally retarded that concerned me. She connected things that had no link and dismissed what needed connecting. She reminded me often, "My son isn't going to take it well how you made the baby that way."

What she didn't know was that I had already told him over the phone about the baby. Initially, I didn't sense it was a problem. But when his mother started saying things like "the baby had twelve toes because Nusrat's parents are cousins and that Yvonne was retarded," I decided to get her checked. In my heart, I knew she was perfect. I just needed a doctor to agree and put an end to Mrs. Brown's terrible accusations. After several examinations, the doctors concluded: "Yvonne Brown is a bright and happy baby. She enjoys nursing from the mother's abundant milk supply. There is no evidence of mental retardation."

⊱ ⊰

It was the end of May and almost a month and a half after Yvonne was born when Curtis came home unannounced. He came straight to our room where he found me appearing to nap in the bed and Yvonne sleeping in the crib. Both excited and exhausted to see him, I faked sleep to watch how he would react to his baby. It was like he melted at the sight of her the same way I did. She began to stir and instead of rubbing her or kissing her, he walked over to my side of the bed. He dropped his jeans in front of me and nudged me to wake. My eyes widened with shock, I immediately looked the other way at the crib.

"Is the baby sleeping?" I asked.

"She's fine." He gently stroked my hair. "Did you miss me?"

I was put off by the way he announced himself without any warning of his arrival. I replied, "Maybe."

His lips became razor straight. "*Maybe?*"

He put his hand up as if to slap me in the face. I flinched and drew my eyes to the ground.

"Well, *maybe* you thought I forgot about what you and your goddamn Iranian family did to my daughter!"

"Curtis!" I looked up in despair and disbelief that he would hit me. "What do you *mean?* The baby is *fine!*" My voice crumbled with desperation. "You weren't even here!"

He put it in my face.

"What's this? I'm sorry Curtis, but she's beautiful, isn't she? And she's healthy. I have all the paperwork that says so."

"Beautiful," he said as he calmed down and softened to my willing mouth. "Yvonne looks just like you Nusrat."

He cupped his left hand behind my neck pulling me forward with force. He then shoved the black strings of hair from my eyes and traced the mascara that smeared down my cheek.

When he finished, Curtis fell asleep on my stomach. I turned myself to the right and pushed him in the opposite direction where he slumped into sleep. *Thank God Yvonne was still asleep.* With my back to him, I closed my eyes and did what I thought any respectable wife would do under these circumstances: fantasize about a man who made me feel anything but pain. I saw the security guard's face in the light of my mind. I imagined how delicate he would be with me as he peeled away my delicate petals. At the same time, I took the memory of Curtis' new-found force and kept it in one chamber of my exhausted heart.

The next day, I mailed my parents a letter informing them that we would be bringing their first-born grandchild in a few weeks. I also revealed my satisfaction with married life and the joys of becoming a mother (nothing farther from the truth).

Untying herself from the rope, a camel drinks before returning home. A baby prepares for traveling after pre-existence. Nursing from the breast, I'm relaxed. Nothing is as it seems.

CHAPTER EIGHT

We arrived in Tehran at the beginning of June 3, 1977. I could finally breathe. Takoma Park and Mrs. Brown were now so far away. However, my return had not eliminated the elders' suspicions or distrust of my husband. If anything, they had increased. Just as Curtis and I planned, we brought two-month-old Yvonne to meet her Iranian family and more importantly we came to Iran to start our life.

Relieved to be with my parents, I felt the familiarity of peace. I was thrilled watching them swallow the baby up with love. The way in which they waited for the moment Yvonne was finished nursing to finally kiss her entire face, made me happy. The home, in constant rotation of aunties and uncles, was cramped with love. Everyone steadily fussed over who was going to hold her next.

I wasn't expecting the compliments my family gave me about how beautiful motherhood made me look. I didn't view myself as being gorgeous and surely didn't feel that way on the inside. At times, maybe when Curtis touched me, I felt attractive. At this moment, it seemed like days since he had even done that. Consumed with motherhood and being a wife, my new priorities barely gave me time to look at my face in a mirror let alone continue my regular beauty regiments. I didn't feel "beautiful" and was grateful that the feelings of exhaustion weren't apparent on my face.

My father hugged me tightly in his arms, "Nusrat Joon, it's so good to see my beautiful daughter and her little one."

And then a flash of disdain glazed my heart. I remembered the last time Curtis called me "beautiful." It was when he saw Yvonne for the first time. Then Maman inspected me from head to toe in admiration as if visiting America had improved my appearance somehow.

"I see you're wearing one of the tailored maternity tunics I mailed you. Nusrat Joon, you look so chic."

After I gave birth, it became clearer to me how I inherited Maman's understanding of using apparel to elevate one's appearance. I made the best use of my maternity clothes after the baby by paring my tailored tunics with a skirt instead of slacks. I believed wearing pants drew unwanted attention to my wide hips. Taking an objective and realistic look in deciding how to conceal my postpartum belly, I wore a black knee-length A-line skirt with a black tunic gracing my full bosom with a white silk scarf. I was pleased to know Maman liked my well thought out ensemble. It was a perfect time to tell her that I hadn't returned home empty-handed. "I brought you several pieces of fine lingerie from a fancy place called Lord and Taylor," I said in her ear. "Curtis and I packed everything we thought you'd like from spices to vitamins. We even brought some books on politics for Baba." Watching her face light up, I called my husband to bring the suitcase. My parents unzipped the suitcase and all of the gifts fell out onto the floor. They went through each item, including the Tabasco sauce and delighted in each piece as a prized American treasure.

It was a warm occasion, my parents probably thought, and the arrival of their first grandchild was more than likely to right all the wrongs in their universe. We weren't in the house for fifteen minutes when Maman and Baba went into their room and returned with something in hand. "Here Nusrat Joon. This is from us."

They placed five twenty-four karat gold bangles on my left wrist and a sapphire necklace around my neck. It didn't stop there. The baby was showered with gifts: handmade blankets, Pahlavi coins, and my favorite, a set of solid twenty-four karat gold anklets with bells. Maman said, "Nusrat, we can't wait to hear Yvonne Joon walk around the house and hear the little sound of the bells jingling about her ankles!"

On our second day back home, still recovering from jetlag, I craved Maman's tea to aid me in waking up. I joined my parents in the kitchen while the baby slept and Curtis ran errands. Sipping the tea, I took in the aroma of the cardamom and closed my eyes over the cup for a brief moment. The tea was delicious, and so was the feeling of home. The cup, which was imported from Bombay, part of a complete set, was a gift to Maman from her in-laws. The set was an ivory color and included a small floral design of pink roses. It reminded me of when my parents remarried. Taking another sip, I returned my attention to my parents. My father, handsome as always, appeared to have more wrinkles on his forehead. My mother, still short and overweight, was losing the glimmer in her eyes. I hoped that I wasn't overly critical, but I feared my mother's diabetes was getting worse. Taking care of Maman and worrying about me in America looked like it took a toll on Baba physically and emotionally.

Maman placed three oranges, one at a time, in a blue bowl on the table. Baba was reading the newspaper. I sensed both of them were waiting for me to talk. I felt like they were fearful of initiating a conversation and appearing nosy. My eyes wandered to my almost empty cup. To my left, Maman brought the kettle to pour more tea. Across the table, I caught Baba peering over his newspaper to read my face.

Baba said, "Curtis left this morning to run errands, eh? He's coming back soon?"

Quite often, Baba asked questions instead of making statements. But everyone knew he was making a statement especially when he added "eh." I knew his motive was to get me to take advantage of the little alone time we had to have a candid conversation. I put my cup down, cleared my throat and said, "He..."

They looked at each other and eagerly gave me their undivided attention.

"He doesn't care about me." I looked down at the table for a second, and then brought my eyes back up to meet theirs, "This is the problem in our marriage."

"What do you *mean* he *doesn't* care for you?" Maman asked.

"He has a good job, he makes a lot of money, and he gave you a child," Baba added.

"What more could you want?" Maman protested.

"He wasn't there when I gave birth. How *could* he care about *me?*"

"He was working here, Nusrat Joon." Maman got up to sit beside me. "That's why." She rubbed my back. "He was providing for *you* and the baby."

"No, I can't accept that. I never had a baby before and he left me in America with his mother. His boss offered him time off, but he chose not to come back."

"Don't be so emotional," Baba insisted. "He loves you, Nusrat. You're acting as if he beats you."

I wanted to tell them how I feared he was capable of beating me, but I couldn't bring myself to reveal this painful truth. They would be devastated.

"I gave birth to Yvonne in April and he didn't see her until May when he just popped up out of nowhere."

I wondered if they were even listening to me.

"I was alone with my child and his wicked mother. What did I do to have such luck?"

"Don't speak ill of your mother-in-law, she did her best," Baba said.

"*Did her best?*" I shook my head in disbelief. "She did her *best* to treat me horribly. You wouldn't believe me if I told you that she starved me while I was pregnant. She gave me only crackers and water."

My chest tightened.

"Did you hear me? Crackers and water! Thank goodness Yvonne is healthy, but it's *not* because of that woman."

Though I could tell my parents listened to every word I said, they acted as if they couldn't believe Curtis would permit anyone to mistreat me in such a way. How foolish was I to think I could tell them anything? I had known better. I knew they believed women could sometimes make more of their situation due to being emotional creatures. Especially me, their daughter, who always had big ideas of putting education and a career before a family.

"In his country, they *don't* see me. They only see *him*. He wasn't even there when his daughter was born and he *still* had the power to name her. I specifically told the nurse that her name was to be Yvonne Nardin Brown, but she didn't listen to me," I pointed to myself. "The woman that just had a cesarean section with an eight-pound baby. No, the nurse listened to a man who chose his job over his daughter's birth and why does he get away with it all? Why? Because he's American."

"In the end, you got the name you wanted right?" Maman asked.

"Yes. After I had to learn how to go to the place in Baltimore for Yvonne's social security card, I had to also get the name changed by myself. Taking a bus from here, taking the train to there. You don't know how hard it was for me to get around."

"He's here with you now."

Baba must have thought he was making a valid point to mention the obvious.

"Isn't he? Yes, and that's all that matters."

"Did you just hear anything I said to you?" Completely aggravated, I raised my voice, "How can I expect either of you to understand? You," I looked at Maman, "married Baba when you were eleven and then drove him away from us to the point where he left for India. I grew up not even knowing him. You constantly moved me back and forth from Bombay, Iran, Iraq and then back to Bombay. I'm glad you've finally planted yourselves back here in Iran, but it was difficult for me. Yes, I learned several languages and grew cultured. But, I never had rights anywhere, and here I am with the same problem again. You taught me the positive things about traveling, but in reality, when you change a place, you have to start all over. I don't want that for my child. I want her to have stability in her life. I want her to stay in *one* place and start her roots."

The more I told them about what was really going on, the more I saw they didn't believe me. For a moment, I was stung by the memory of Curtis' raised hand to my face as he forced himself on me and called me a "foreigner." I wanted to cry, to be able to release the pressure in my throat that came from the breaking in my heart. Only my eyes (which I was sure were swelling and glossy by now) could foretell that I was about to explode. Never expecting the tsunami of emotions to creep out, I cried, "I'm *scared* of him!"

Like water breaking free from a dam, my tears gushed uncontrollably. I couldn't believe what I just confessed.

"The man that we all love."

I couldn't control my voice from stuttering in between catching my breath.

"The one that can do no wrong ..."

I cringed at the thought of allowing my parents to believe what they wanted. The record had to be set straight.

"He put his hand to my face as if to nearly slap me to the floor!"

"We do *not* believe it, Nusrat." Baba retorted. "We want you to stay with us, but you do *not* have to go about it this way. Work on your marriage. It isn't easy, but it will work out."

I slumped in my chair, put my head down on the table, and felt my heart break all over again.

"Do you think," I paused and wiped tears from my eyes. "Do you think," I steadied my voice, "Do you think I'm making this up just to stay in your home?"

"No, we just want what's best for you," Maman said. "Of course you can stay here. We would love for you and your family to be here. You don't have to go about it in this manner is all we're saying."

"You want what is best for who? It sounds to me you're with Curtis." The heavy weight of defeat loomed over my whole body. "I'm *your* daughter. Why don't you believe *me*? Why would *I* lie?"

⤟⤞

After living with my parents for two months, Curtis got a new job as a contractor for Lockheed Martin. Finally, it was time, I thought, for the three of us to move into our own place. Limited space and my parents siding with him made things unbearable. That night when he came home from work and ate his dinner, I complained to him about how my parents were interfering with how I was taking care of the baby. I didn't know how he would respond, but at this point, I figured it was worth a shot. I suggested we seriously discuss our housing options and then I just came out and asked, "Don't you think it's time that we are together, just the three of us?"

"Sure. Why not? If it will make you happy, let's do it."

"Great!" I kissed him on the lips. Yes, I was shocked by his reaction, but maybe it was his way of sorting out his guilt and making things better between us. We both agreed we would eventually purchase a home in northern Iran and that an apartment, for now, seemed more practical. "I think I saw a *for rent* sign at an apartment a couple of blocks away! I'll look into it tomorrow while you're at work."

That night, I couldn't wait to tell my parents how we had decided to move out. I imagined how I would rub it in their faces just a little bit. Once again, I was gaining my independence. Now, the power in Maman's voice would be forced to subside. Maman exuded the kind of pushy dominance that almost always accompanied the "living with parents" arrangement. It always started innocently with words like, "Oh, my dear Nusrat and Curtis, we think it's best that you all stay with us until you can get on your feet," then it transformed into sporadic digs about parental irresponsibility and how "your relationship would be better if..."

It was now time to enact the scenario that had consistently replayed in my mind as of late. I awoke at around nine o'clock to a quiet house as Curtis had already left for work. I picked Yvonne from the crib, nursed and changed her, and then headed to the kitchen to prepare break-fast. My parents were already drinking tea. "Good morning Maman and Baba," I said as I glided through the kitchen to give them both a kiss. But their responses broke my stride; I noticed their withdrawn faces and felt a broken heartedness about them. I instantly felt a pang of guilt. It dissolved as quickly as it came. My father was praying with his string of beads in hand and Maman was rocking back and forth praying. "Why so grim, I have good news to share," I said as I tried to contain my excite-ment. "We have decided to move into our own place. I'm going to work on my marriage just like *you* advised."

It was as if Maman and Baba were in a distant place in their indi-vidual minds. I knew they heard me, but neither of them responded.

"Did you hear me?"

They both nodded "yes" while Baba repeated his prayer at just above a whisper. It eerily sounded like a repetitive chant he did when upset and Maman just continued rocking. Finally, Maman spoke, "Your father had a terrible nightmare."

She made eye contact with him as if to telepathically command him to share the details. He followed the order, "The earth shook. The pots clanged against each other and fell off the walls. I was completely terri-fied. I ran to the front door, so wobbly was the ground that I had a hard time making my way. When I got to the door, I cracked it open and saw a large hole in the earth. I looked down in the deep pit and saw noth-ing but infinite darkness. When I opened the door completely, voices as if shouts and screams came to me and when I closed the door there was only silence. Across a field, what seemed a world away, you stood on the gutted edge of a rock clutching the baby as if your life depended on it. Curtis stood behind you looking like the devil himself. His eyes were dark like the gargoyles I've seen in London. He had a grin so sin-ister that I lost my breath. I could hear your voice. At first, it sounded jumbled, but then it became coherent. 'Help me!' You said, yet your lips didn't move. It was as if you were speaking to me through your mind. In an instant, you were gone. I felt so helpless. I woke up and immediately prayed. There was nothing else I could do."

I had to ask, "Was Yvonne alright?"

"Yes, all three of you were fine," Baba said as he clung to his prayer beads.

"I'm sure it's nothing serious Baba. Please don't worry yourself."

"It was real you know? It vexes my spirit so."

He examined my eyes as if to find an explanation or the translation of the visions. "I understand you want to move, I'm not sure if it's the wisest decision, but I understand the desire to be independent. We're the ones who cultivated this spirit in you. So if you want to bloody move, you have my blessing."

Whenever Baba used the term "bloody," (his British influenced word of choice when irritated) I knew it was serious.

"But we aren't moving far, just a few blocks away," I said in an attempt to somehow soften the mood. "Please don't panic and worry. We're going to be fine, I promise you."

⚒ ⚒

On August 1, 1977, Curtis secured the apartment and we moved in. With so many life events and transitions, I desired to center myself and find balance. Instead of a housewarming party, I decided to have a sofreh, making it a religious event and invited only the women in my family. Starting a new chapter in our first place was significant cause to gather in prayer to promote blessings and a peaceful life. To say things got better with Curtis when we moved to our own place wouldn't be a complete lie. In fact, sparing Yvonne from Mrs. Brown and no longer living with the stress of my parents siding with her father was a big relief. Now that we no longer lived with them, I would have to become adjusted to the notion of *my* own family. From the bottom of my heart, I knew this was not going to be without pitfalls.

Living in our own space, I soon learned how I didn't share in a number of my husband's interests, especially a recent past time he picked up while I was pregnant in the U.S. - *gambling*. I couldn't accept how people could enjoy risking what they had worked so hard to gain. I had known of others who had taken up this hobby. What upset me were their eyes, how their gaze took on a surreal look as if all time had been suspended. Only the gambler and the idea of "rainbow chasing" took precedence over reality. I saw this in Curtis and became uneasy at his growing impatience as it spilled over into every aspect of his being. However difficult, I had grown to live on edge in his presence. His easily changeable mood now dictated by what felt like constant unpredictability, made me wonder the significant role his mother's evil had played on his behavior. Living with Mrs. Brown had opened my eyes to Curtis' childhood. It also made me more sympathetic to his upbringing. His mother was, in fact, the culprit to his new behavior in our marriage. For this reason, I vowed to help him return to the charming man I knew he was deep down inside. I hadn't come this far with him to give up now.

I decided to try and understand his idiosyncrasies as a discerning wife should. I whole-heartedly believed in the sanctity of my wedding vows. I kept it in my mind that Allah favored the dutiful wife. So when Curtis' habit of leaving the bathroom door open as he read the paper and paraded around the house in nothing more than his briefs disgusted me, I bit my tongue. I envisioned the good qualities that I had known existed. It wasn't long before I began to question the life I was accustomed to in which men and women being covered in front of each other was a cultural norm. Whether married or not, men, as well as women, didn't dare walk around the house exposing themselves in such an indecent manner. Baba was always fully covered in the house. It was embarrassing when Curtis did it and I found myself staring at the floor so as to not look at him directly. I think he must have taken this as a show of my submissiveness and *his* dominance.

I was shy at first in showing my body, but I slowly felt comfortable being nude outside the bed. It was a necessary act I performed to show I was letting my guard down, softening to my husband. I had stopped putting my robe on to walk to the bathroom that was a relatively short distance from the bedroom. He would tease me when I'd look in his direction to see if he was staring at my body. Laughing at me, he'd say, "I've seen everything already Nusrat. You're my wife, don't you know? And I love the view!"

Now that I had grown accustomed to my husband's crude wit, I hoped he found me attractive again. But when he came into the bathroom to use the toilet while I was in the shower, the smell of his waste repulsed me as I washed my body. It was like the horrible odor choked the life out of the floral fragrance of my soap. *What a pig. What kind of man did I marry?* This wasn't exactly the life I had dreamed of, but I was dedicated to making it work.

Another aspect that took getting used to was our marital relations in the bedroom. The thunderous passion we once embodied on the beaches of the Caspian Sea was now a thing of the past. Things were no longer the same. I was no longer a career woman or just someone's daughter. Rarely did I miss working, but when I did, I wondered how our relationship would be if I returned. In any event, my heart was at home raising my baby. I was giving Yvonne the best I had to offer in time, love, and care. I had my hands full with new responsibilities and considered myself lucky.

With the beginning of autumn, my days became filled with sewing, making torshi (pickled vegetables), walking back and forth to the minimarket, preparing fresh food, and nursing Yvonne. When I had a few spare minutes, I jotted down my thoughts in my journal. I wrote on topics relating to my experience as a new mother and now homemaker. Sometimes I wrote a few lines of poetry here and there often leaving them unfinished. What I was able to express revealed the ever-growing emptiness in my heart and the desire to rekindle my short-lived love affair with my husband. Secretly, I had hoped he would find my journal and be inspired to turn things all around.

It wasn't long before I established a friendship with my neighbor, Mrs. Shirazi, who often boasted about her son's position at the Department of Energy: "My son can turn on and off the power in the entire country!"

Despite Mrs. Shirazi's annoying praise of her son, I respected her for taking care of her sick grandchild who required dialysis. She was funny in that it didn't matter to her that I was married. She wanted me for her son and didn't hold back her real thoughts. She said to me, "I see your husband leaving in the morning to go to work. It's just that my son's wife died during childbirth and he needs someone loving like you in his life.

I see how you are with your daughter. I smell the fresh food you cook daily. And you're elegant clothes, you're so beautiful. With all the money my son has, he needs someone like you too."

"Thank you, Mrs. Shirazi, but Yvonne loves her father dearly." Just as I'd respond, I knew it wouldn't stop her from convincing me about her son again.

Mrs. Shirazi made me feel revitalized with her generous compliments. I only wished I had heard them from my husband. It made me realize how visiting America taught me how much Iranians embraced the western style of fashion. On the whole, I viewed my taste to be more ethnic than western except for when it came to my natural curly hair, which I worked hard to straighten. Now with a little more time to take care of myself, I religiously rolled my hair hoping to train it to be full and straight. I liked my hair to be elevated on the top to give the illusion of height. Standing at five foot one, I tried desperately to do what I could to appear taller. The key for me was to make everything look effortless.

At last, I returned to the art of creating the perfect eyebrow. It was etched in my grooming habits and I missed it so much with taking care of the baby. Once again, tweezers and a mirror floated around the house for when I needed to catch a stray hair before the follicle budded. My eyebrows, arched with precision, drew attention to my eyes. My makeup was light and natural mostly. When I wanted to be fancy for Curtis, I'd dramatize my eyes with heavy black eyeliner and mascara like Elizabeth Taylor had done as Cleopatra. It surprised me that Mrs. Shirazi noticed me. Did she see me as exotic because of my American husband? Did I appear western or unique? I didn't realize that I had stood out that much. Were these the things that made me stand out in her eyes?

That November and December in 1977, President Carter and the Shah visited each other in their respected countries. Consumed with work, Curtis was more interested in making money than with affairs of the home. I prayed the gambling had subsided. I focused on stabilizing my family, but I wanted a home, not an apartment and this was on my radar to accomplish. Sometimes when he was in a relaxed mood, he took Yvonne to his chest and rocked her to sleep. At ten months old, she was at a substantial size for him to feel at ease handling her in the kitchen sink. One day he put her in the inflatable tub and for the first time, he bathed his daughter. At first, he ate up her wiggles and laughter. But when he went to wash her little toes, he acted as if he was triggered to the hate he had for me all over again.

"Goddamn it Nusrat! Your family did this to her! How are we supposed to find shoes to fit her? She can't wear flip-flops in the snow! Or for the rest of her life!"

Every chance he got, he blamed my family for "handicapping" our daughter. One day I was his beautiful wife and the next I was like a hideous beast prompted by his glance at Yvonne's extra toes. How could he let this issue be an element of division in our marriage? Before the child was born, he knew of my parents being first cousins, something normal in the days of them growing up in Iran. But it was a fact clouded by his thoughts of me initially being beautiful like Maman. He no longer saw our faces as mere coincidence. No, for Curtis, our faces were now a result of what he viewed as inbreeding and so were Yvonne's toes. Never mind what the doctor had said about our daughter being "normal."

When he would shout at me, I felt that it was just a matter of time that he would strike me down. Outside of serving him meals, I kept my distance. To avoid an argument, I chose to exclusively wash Yvonne. I took special care in keeping her feet covered with either socks or a blanket. Under so much strain from trying to please him and consistently failing to convert this difficult situation into something agreeable, my hate for Curtis deepened.

Our marriage went on like this while unrest among various anti-West groups who were against the Shah flourished. If only the two sides could appreciate my peace strategy where the necessity of compromise was guided by understanding. Then in all probability, the events that were about to take place would more than likely not have taken up chapters in the history books yet to be written.

CHAPTER NINE

Throughout Iran, several demonstrations against the Shah and Western ideologies took place between January and March of 1978. The everyday hardships of my life in Tehran were dramatized by the quickly changing political landscape. When Norouz arrived, Curtis invited my parents and a handful of extended family to celebrate. For weeks I shopped and prepared for the event, cleaning and purifying our home of negative energy. It was the first time he initiated any family gathering like this since we were married. With my family actively engaged in the American holidays with Christmas gifts and celebrating the American New Year, Curtis must have thought it was appropriate to finally reciprocate. But for no reason or warning, he abruptly canceled the festivities the day before. He cautioned me, "You better tell them that it's called off."

Another one of his crazy behaviors, I thought, more grief that I had to manage. "I have to do this when there's no reason for it?"

"Figure it out."

"But we can't do this. It just *doesn't* happen like that."

And he never gave me a reason for his actions. He knew I was fuming with embarrassment with every call. If I didn't know better, I'd think he loved seeing me hurt.

"We can't always have our way now *can* we?" He said.

"You sound like your mother now," I responded. "This is our holiday, it's not about me having my way. Do you hate me?"

His behavior didn't make sense. His revenge came for no reason. My emptiness deepened. Nevertheless, I still set the sofreh, a ceremonial table adorned with symbolic items for Yvonne to enjoy. I caught a glimpse of myself in the sofreh mirror and saw a tired face. On Norouz, I was about to dissect every line, dark circle, and hair on my face, but then Maman called, "Eid Mubarak Nusrat. Put the phone to Yvonne Joon's ear."

I held the phone to Yvonne's ear as she grabbed for the cord to put in her mouth. She smiled at the sound of Maman's voice. I made sure Curtis wasn't in earshot and returned to speaking, "Maman, I'm so sorry about what he did." I lowered my voice. "I don't know why he does these things."

"This is what a man is Nusrat. They're all like this. You think it's only your husband?"

I knew Maman was trying to make me feel better by minimizing the magnitude of Curtis' act. But it didn't alleviate the sting I felt from his joy of embarrassing me. "I see. This is something difficult for me. I don't know how to forgive him this time. It's like he delights in making me suffer."

"Maybe the demonstrations in Tabriz have affected him? How does he feel about the anti-West sentiment?"

I imagined the far-fetched possibility of Curtis being affected by the demonstrators. That thought came and went quickly. "He never talks about it. I don't see this being the issue. I think he just hates me because of Yvonne's feet; it's his way of retaliating against us somehow. But we'll never fully know the truth I guess. He tells me what he wants and keeps the rest to himself. I'm left clueless."

The following month, a beautiful flower-filled April, my parents insisted on having Yvonne's first birthday at their home. Another disappointment, Curtis showed up late making work as the excuse. This time, I managed to focus on the beauty of the moment with my baby and family anyway. Yvonne wore an orange silk dress with matching orange socks. I sat her on my lap in front of the birthday cake. There she was, a doll full of smiles and joy, clapping with her little hands while everyone sang "Happy Birthday." This would be the last joyous occasion for my family and me to share. The sound of my parents singing to Yvonne would soon become an echo in my ear.

For me, the earliest evidence that the opposition was on the rise and hitting closer to home was at the beginning of August 1978. I had seen some young men set a tire on fire. At the time, Curtis cautioned me not to worry and then on the morning of August 20th, I took Yvonne to visit my parents and things became grimly clear. As soon as I entered the home, Maman greeted us with a dart of panic, "Nusrat! Are you okay? Is Yvonne okay?"

Standing before her, we were fine, but Maman insisted on dissecting us from head to toe. It was like she was making sure we looked the same.

"Of course we're okay. What's wrong Maman? Did something happen?"

"We just learned on the television set that the Cinema Rex theater showing the film Gavaznha (The Deer) burnt down killing hundreds of people."

"Oh my! Why? How did it burn down?"

"Not exactly sure, it's completely devastating." Baba's voice lowered. "They say the exit doors were locked which means all those people were trapped, left to burn away like nothing."

"Great! Maybe this is Allah's way of telling me that Curtis will get killed!"

"This is no laughing matter Nusrat. This is serious and it means something else bigger will follow. If you want to see him suffer, then divorce." Baba said as easy as he could.

I wasn't surprised. Divorcing my husband never entered my mind. Raising Yvonne without the benefit of a father was unfathomable. It wasn't an option and yet I didn't know what was. Baba continued talking. "It won't take long for Islamic fundamentalists and the SAVAK, the Shah's secret police, to point fingers of blame at each other for this incident. It won't be good. I don't know what's happening to our country."

Then Maman's words came into my mind. I remembered when I was a child and she was searching for Baba. The first moment she got, she pleaded with him, "Nusrat needs you!"

Thank Allah he had agreed. The memory of my first day of kindergarten came to me and how during lunch-time, the smell of fresh pita bread filled the air. All I could think of was eating it. No one gave me lunch. I sat with nothing before me and watched my teacher and classmates eat. I worked so hard to avoid their eyes as my belly rumbled. I was too young to understand how my Iranian identity was the reason for their ill treatment towards me. My parents pulled me out of that school the same day. They enrolled me in a private school with hopes it would lessen the burden of being a foreigner. I couldn't live with myself if Yvonne faced a similar fate due to her American citizenship. She needed her father too. At the same time, I couldn't see her in Mrs. Brown's arms. With all of her racial issues, I couldn't let her poison my child's mind.

Maman started yelling at me, so I gave her my undivided attention.

"With all the protesters killed in Isfahan and the Cinema Rex fire, you aren't scared? They hate Americans Nusrat! You don't think this can be dangerous for Curtis? For the baby? Are *you* mad? Pack up and move with us! What are you waiting for?"

Baba interjected, "Here, you're all safe and protected. Living there, you never know when the next demonstration will happen. Our guards and gates provide security. Your mother is right. You should return."

And here I was in a similar predicament like when I was a child. But, I wasn't going to do what Maman did to me. I wasn't going to divorce to remarry. I wasn't going to let people mistreat Yvonne. I was going to make it work with Curtis. I *needed* to believe things would eventually improve.

⊨⊹ ⊹⊨

As an act of revolt on the government, Mrs. Shirazi's son, who was publicly pro-revolution, cut off the power on the hottest day in August. Just days after the Cinema Rex fire. This act affected hospitals, airports, my apartment, and he had even hurt his son who needed the electricity for dialysis. The revolution was becoming more real and it quickly intensified. Luckily, the next day, power returned and we had lights again. Seizing the moment, I sat Yvonne in the baby bouncer and entered the kitchen to prepare dinner and saw the lights flicker in the apartment. Washing the chicken in the sink, I thought Mrs. Shirazi's son would cut off the power until the light blinked a few times more finally staying completely lit. Suddenly I felt angry. Angry with my marriage, the bombings, at the demonstrators, angry with Mrs. Shirazi's son, at the piece of chicken I didn't know was going to get cooked or not, I was angry at *everything*. I considered grabbing the baby and going across the hall to Mrs. Shirazi's apartment door to tell her just what I thought about her stupid son. With the lights going out again, I picked up a flashlight and walked across the hall with Yvonne on my hip. Just as I expected, Mrs. Shirazi asked who it was before she opened the door. When the door opened, I blew up.

"We can't live like this anymore! Tell your son to STOP!!!"

"Go to the hell! You're the one that married the American!"

Just before the door slammed shut in my face, I caught a glimpse of her frail grandson hooked up to dialysis. In the seconds our eyes met, the boy's despair penetrated me and it would be a look I could never forget.

With the lights on again, I resumed cooking the food putting my energy into cutting the chicken into chunks for fesenjoon. I wanted to forget what Mrs. Shirazi said about me marrying an American. Yes, he wasn't the best husband, but he certainly wasn't the cause of the political upheaval.

The country's situation intensified that September as our relationship was tempered by Curtis spending so much time at work. With growing hostility towards the West by many Iranians and the public proclamations of "death to America," an unseen strain was forming. Yet, all we had was each other to survive. The power outages became increasingly longer and more consistent. The cool nights became both a source of discomfort and alarm. From the balcony, I saw men shouting "Allah Wakbar!" A look of alarm frequently passed over Yvonne's eyes when she heard their yelling. Even still, returning to my parents' gated community wasn't an option.

To add to that, it became second nature for me to monitor my reactions to her father's behavior in her presence. The same was true when something from outside alarmed me. I wholeheartedly believed that even at her young age, not being able to talk or walk, that all this had affected her mentally. Just thinking about it tore away at me. I saw the government changing to a pro-communist stance making it difficult for me to imagine Yvonne growing up in such an environment. During these episodes, I always made sure the baby was in my arms to distract her from the explosive sounds from the outside. I honestly didn't know what I was going to do. It was difficult to imagine. It was like deciding which poison to drink. Should we stay in our apartment or return to my parents?

Those opposing the Shah were growing in number as evidenced by the sea of people demonstrating in the streets and the universities. The government's response to this was martial law, a curfew to control the rising opposition. The military took over the streets, threatening to shoot on sight anyone who came out after curfew. Enormous T-72 tanks surfaced at the universities in an attempt to regain order. Although the routes of the demonstrations were a considerable distance away, I saw sporadic groups of youths hovered over more tire-burning bonfires. This was enough to fill our lives with chaos and disruption. That October from Iraq, Ayatollah Khomeini urged actions against the Shah which further intensified the opposition's strength and determination. By November, Iran was still under military rule to restore order. But it was evident that order wasn't possible when Iranian soldiers were even going against the Shah. What was happening to my country?

At the beginning of December, the weather was freezing and our whole apartment, no more than eight hundred square feet, was hard to heat without electricity. I didn't know how some of our neighbors were surviving without it. To keep warm, Curtis had purchased kerosene from a nearby gas station to put into a portable heater in our bedroom. From the bed, I watched him pour it carefully. Under five wool blankets and one sheet, I hoped to warm the bed and Yvonne with my body heat until he came to sleep. For a moment, I felt like this was the kind of intimacy I thought I wanted. Nestled in between my baby and husband, I felt warm and cold at the same time. The room had yet to heat up, but the closeness of the moment sparked an odd feeling I didn't think was possible. And there we were, the three of us piled underneath a mountain of blankets in the dark, having only each other for heat and survival.

Unlike my parents, who had lived through wars and political strife, I didn't know what it meant to survive it. And Curtis, of course, no stranger to the perils of war, appeared to remain calm which confused me a little. Was he calm because he was trained for extreme circumstances? Or was he the face of "American Arrogance" in which could be heard chanted daily by demonstrators in almost every part of the country? In a briefly extended moment, a new feeling of unrest crept into my mind. I feared Curtis' manner implied some form of involvement.

"Curtis?" I startled him to wake.

"It's going to be okay."

He assured me and I desperately wanted to believe him. "What's happening?"

Yvonne, nestled between us burst into tears in her sleep as if she was tortured by the atmosphere. Her increased nightmares ripped at my soul. I comforted her with kisses and rubbed her forehead until she went back to sleep.

"Not sure. I don't have the car and driver anymore. Lockheed is preparing to evacuate."

"To where?"

"The U.S."

I heard his words as if given a terminal diagnosis. I laid in the darkness. The smell from the kerosene was making me cough. The cold didn't matter anymore or if the heater exploded - I was in shock. I knew if the Americans were preparing to evacuate the country for what they perceived was an imminent situation, then surely Curtis would return to America and would expect me and Yvonne to follow. But returning to the U.S. meant seeing his mother and this was too much for me to bear. I didn't want my daughter's identity sabotaged before it fully came to be. My sense of the future hung by an eyelash of a chance. I didn't say another word out loud and silently prayed: *O Allah, please guide me in the right way. Please bestow your generous mercy upon us and provide me with the wisdom to do what is right and not in haste.*

Curtis' words disrupted me in mid-prayer. "We will drop Yvonne off with your parents in the morning and go to the consulate to get your visa."

The next morning we caught a cab to my parents' home and then headed to the consulate. The snow from the previous day had already melted from the morning sun. This was the cycle of the current winter, not treacherous like past winters in Tehran. It was Tuesday morning and the highest temperature of the day was expected to be forty degrees, yet I felt beads of sweat on my forehead. My thoughts were racing as to what was about to unfold. Going to the consulate meant that returning to America was a reality. Outside my window, I saw an elderly woman carrying a bag and trying to get our driver's attention to stop and pick her up. In Farsi, I told the cab driver not to miss her. Curtis glared at me. I saw his eyes ready to burst into an irrational explosion.

"Never mind, she can catch the next cab," I said.

I had seen that look before we got married, but didn't trust my instincts then. Now it was clear. I married the devil, just as Baba had dreamed. And his American nationality was not a plus. Instantly, my heart raced, and I felt like I was choking on my breath. Returning to America was about to become my reality. I had to do something. And then a force came over me that I had never experienced.

"No." I said aloud and thankful no one had heard me. I closed my eyes fighting off the images of Mrs. Brown not welcoming me into her home, talking so disrespectful about me and hearing her say, "You're a foreigner!" I shook back and forth in a quick manner as if to release the thoughts. In seconds, I absorbed every mean act from Curtis and his mother that it made me nearly faint. Just watching him look out the window made me sick.

Did he think I was going to let him take me back to the U.S. just so he and his mother could enjoy breaking me down to nothing? Did he expect me to accept all this ill fortune with grace?

The cab driver slowed down near a crowded intersection to pick up the elderly woman. As the wheels rolled to what would be an eventual stop, I quickly grabbed the door handle, turned it open, and ran into the street almost losing my footing in the process.

When I hit the cold concrete, I took off running as fast as I could in the opposite direction. I wasn't thinking, only running away from him so that I could return to my parent's home and get Yvonne. What was I going to do then? It didn't matter, I had to get away from Curtis. The cold December air overpowered my face as I ran against the wind further away from the cab. Cigarette smoke from a nearby homeless man reciting Ferdowsi in front of a clothing boutique trapped my airways for seconds until I coughed.

"Wait! Stop! Stop the cab." I heard Curtis, but dared not turn to face him. "Stay here!" He shouted at the cab driver and then I heard his voice drawing closer to me, "Nusrat!"

Sweat poured down my face as I ran past a group of men standing on the curb. Slipping a glance over my shoulder to see if he was truly in pursuit, I ran directly into a police officer. The officer grabbed my shirt to keep me from running and instead we both tumbled onto the ground.

"Help me!" I reached for his arm as he began to get up and move in my direction.

"What is wrong with you!" He said sharply. "Didn't you see me standing here, you idiot, shame on you!"

The officer snatched me as if to hold me until Curtis caught up with us. I peered at the officer to do something, to see my vulnerability, to have compassion.

"Thank you, sir," Curtis muttered. Clenching my left wrist, he said, "I knew I couldn't trust you."

Pulling my hand out from his hold, my wedding ring had slid off my finger and fell onto the sidewalk. "My ring, Curtis! It fell."

"You're lying."

"Look at my finger, it fell."

Searching for it, he finally saw the ring next to his foot where he almost walked on it. "Here." He put the ring back on my finger. "Now, I'm going to drag your ass back to the cab."

"What's wrong with you? I just want you to love me. I just want you to be a good husband. Is that too much? Look at you. What's all this?"

I felt like I was having an out of body experience where nothing was moving. The women and children in their chadors scared to meet my eyes went out of sight. My eyes wandered to the trees outlining the street, but my perspective was a blur. Soon I caught a distant glimpse of the American Embassy and felt paralyzed. Then for a brief moment, my eyes met Curtis and I saw no mercy, just pure evil. Was this what the elders had seen all along? Why was I so blind?

The spectacle of my dilemma oppressed me like never before. Returning to America meant seeing his mother. I became sick to my stomach. I decided to stay in Iran with my daughter. Curtis could go back to his country. This would be best for all of us. Life in Iran would become all Yvonne would know and the two of us would live in peace far from Curtis and his mother. Overcome with disbelief at the reality unfolding before me, I gazed out the window. And then I noticed a little girl walking down the street. She couldn't have been more than five years old. Her dark almond eyes made me think of Yvonne, and then I envisioned my daughter at the same age growing up in Iran. An unusual calm came over me and with a second thought, I pulled away, but Curtis' grip was too firm.

"I'm not returning with you," I said. I wanted to spit in his face but dared not for fear of what would happen. "Your America can keep her freedom! Get off me! I won't be a slave in your country, in your mother's house, or anywhere!" I opened the door and ran out again.

"Oh, yes you will."

He turned his face in the direction of the cab and then grabbed for my wrist. I ran as fast as I could, but he caught up to me quicker this time. He then pulled me by the ear nearly a hundred feet back to the cab. Like a dog, sadly defeated, but more embarrassed, I was in disbelief that this was happening publicly. The first and last time he did anything like this was in the United States and that was in his bedroom. Now, the pain was open for all to see. Curtis opened the cab's door and like lightning, struck my face. I leaned my head against the window and saw a little girl crying. The rest of the spectators were nothing but blurred fragments. With his show, Curtis had given them their evening's gossip. What a dreadful life.

"Thanks for waiting," Curtis said to the driver. "We're on our way to the consulate. My wife will speak only English now."

What happened next was over in fifteen minutes. The cab driver continued driving and at the second stop, I jumped out again, nearly killing myself in the middle of the road. Curtis jumped out and caught me like he did the first time. His slaps turned to punches. I didn't cry, scream, or hit him back. It was useless. No one would stop him. The average person didn't want to deal with the embarrassment of coming between a husband and wife. By the time we got to the consulate, my face was swollen. I covered up most of it with my scarf before we entered the building. It was strange for me to be totally overpowered by Curtis as if I was nothing. I fulfilled my promise to give him an American child, but I didn't agree to live in the United States. This was never a part of the plan.

He whispered to me, "I'm going to get your visa. If you leave, I will catch you." Pulling my ear close to his mouth he said, "and this time I'll kill you."

Never had I been filled with so much darkness. As I sat in a corner waiting for him to finish, I wanted nothing more than to release the vomit working its way from my stomach to my throat. All I could think of was that I must live long enough to be a good mother for Yvonne. Then, the famous Iranian singer, Hayedeh, entered the room and everyone around looked at her in amazement. I saw her and adored her beauty from afar. My happy younger self would've run up to her asking for an autograph, but my mind was a million miles away. I closed my eyes to pray. I asked Allah for direction and begged for guidance. What seemed like hours were only a few minutes. With my eyes still closed, my face was accidentally exposed and then I heard a voice. I would've thought it was the voice of Allah answering my prayers, but it was a woman.

"You don't deserve it," she said.

I opened my eyes and saw Hayedeh's face.

"My poor crying girl..." She repeated, "No one deserves to be treated like a donkey."

I caught Curtis watching me as if to determine my next move. Hayedeh, left me with one last sentiment, "Freedom is a rose petal many died for my lady."

Her words were a powerful acknowledgment of my current condition. The manner in which I was addressed, as a "poor crying girl," a person I would have never wanted to be, broke my heart.

"Thank you, Ms. Hayedeh." I watched her disappear in the crowd. I put my head back down, "Thank you."

Aside from my nausea, the next day was like none of the madness had ever happened. My life was one big nightmare.

CHAPTER TEN

On January 16, 1979, the Shah and Queen Farah went on "vacation." I couldn't understand why he would leave at such a dangerous time. When would he return? And if he doesn't, who would take over? His son? Russia? The United States? When would the country go back to normal?

Keeping a nationalist stance, my family didn't speak of religion or politics around Curtis. It was their way of balancing tensions. But with everything happening, my questions alone were cause for hysteria. All of this really couldn't be happening. It was just yesterday when Maman and Baba invited everyone in our neighborhood, young and old, to our home. We were all anxious to catch a glimpse of the royal couple on the television set. Our hearts melted in unison at the sight of Queen Farah Diba setting doves free. It was magnificent. And to think at eleven-year's old, I sang the national anthem to her at a school visit. Now, these were all just childhood memories. I had no way of making sense of the turmoil surrounding me. I just wanted to sleep and wake up to a new world free of pain.

Americans in Iran knew they were losing power as American contractors and personnel all over Iran pulled out of the country. What was really happening? Which underground people were going to surface and take over the country? Curtis' supervisors advised him to move us to a more secure location. In a week we moved to a northern part of Iran near a military compound close to the Elahieh neighborhood with an American Marine whose family had already fled. These recent turn of events had made my decision for me. I would raise Yvonne in America and perform my duties as a wife to the best of my abilities. I was and always would be Iranian, unlike my daughter. She would never have the option for dual citizenship under Iranian law since her father was American. Imagining the perilous task ahead of me, I mulled over how I was going to manage my husband's explosive behavior. With so much to consider, I had the presence of mind to sell all of Yvonne's toys, crib, and baby bouncer. All we now had were our clothes, some pistachios, and each other.

On January 30th, 1979, Curtis came home and told me that we had to prepare to leave. "Our names came up on the list of Americans to be evacuated. We've been directed to take one suitcase per person. We don't have time to waste."

I didn't ask questions. We immediately approached the necessary tasks of preparing to leave with ferocious panic. Once more, we were a team as we were when we worked together, working toward a common goal.

That night before Yvonne went to sleep, I waved a diffuser of smoldering black seeds about her head and my own to ward off the evil eye. At midnight, the clock struck. Flinching, I bit my nails and stirred in the bed careful to not wake up Curtis or Yvonne. A solution came to me: I would feed Curtis his favorite meal, provide him sex, put him to sleep and then douse him in gasoline to set him ablaze. That would fix all my problems, right? But then Yvonne wouldn't have a mother. The longer I thought about it, the clearer my destiny unfolded. I wished I had someone to consult with, but it would only make my situation worse. If I stayed in Iran with Yvonne and divorced Curtis, it would be just as bad. Is *this* what Allah wanted?

The most extended hand on the grandfather clock against the vestibule wall was aligned with the twelve while the shortest hand pointed stiffly at the three. It rang in my mind like a booming voice that said "the hour was upon us" and almost instantaneously it was as if the weight of time prevented me from moving. As the minute hand made its way to the beat of the pendulum in slow motion, I knew in my heart that this moment would be forever etched in my mind. I hurriedly forced the last few items of clothing into my suitcase, clamped the two metal clasps, grabbed Yvonne's hand and headed toward the door.

We were to arrive by 4:00 a.m. at the Iranian Air Force base. I became immediately tense with the fact that life would never be the same. The thought of leaving my father, my mother, my grandparents, and my aunties brought dread to my mind. The finality of it all came quickly when we exited the front door and came upon an unusual quiet street.

We boarded a bus headed to a place I didn't know. In minutes, we arrived at what looked like a military base. The driver parked the bus at the corner in front of the commissary where an impromptu line of Americans had been created. We stood there with all our possessions stuffed to capacity in our suitcases awaiting an uncertain future. Jostling in place and rubbing hands together, we desperately tried to remain warm while waiting for other Americans and their families to arrive. I was surprised when I overheard a guard refer to us as evacuees. I suddenly felt like a stranger in my own country. The wait took hours and the horrid collective daydream of a truck filled with former Shah military supporters who had recently jumped ship to join pro-Khomeini groups arriving to mass slaughter our entire group was real in my mind.

I was relieved when the bus pulled up to the curb until I saw the Iranian driver whose eyes faced forward looking intently into the darkness of the morning as if not to meet our eyes, the incoming passengers. His look increased my already uneasiness of having Iranian military escort. The other six soldiers who seemed to magically appear moved about with sharp precision. With AK-47s drawn and pointed in ready-to-shoot positions above us, the apparent lead soldier directed us to board the bus with haste.

Just as soon as the bus had appeared, it sped off surrounded by battle-worn trucks flying small Iranian flags like the motorcade of some prominent political figure or celebrity. Occasionally my eyes met Curtis' with a faint common understanding that for no other reason, returning to America was best for our daughter. By now, I had an odd thought that he somehow knew his temper was getting the best of him and that he wanted to find a way to shield it from me. That was *if* we survived our current situation.

I held Yvonne tightly to my bosom for her tiny frame looked out of place amongst the all-adult group. I whispered a prayer of safety for her sake. My tension was grounded in the thought that if we were to be taken by an Imperial guard conflicted by his political position, my baby would be singled out and punished for being American.

When we arrived at the military airport, we waited in a line to get our documents validated. As if to note Yvonne was the only baby on the trip, the military official smiled at her passport photo before he rushed us along saying, "May Allah bless the child."

His words caught me off guard as he returned her passport to Curtis. Then we were off to where only God knew where. I never could have dreamed of traveling in this covert manner. Curtis promised me that my family was waiting to say farewell there. I hoped he was telling the truth. Under normal circumstances, the three of us would've been given a farewell by a mob of my family. The vision of at least one hundred relatives gathering to scream, cry, embrace, and kiss us goodbye led my eyes to swell with tears.

The feeling that the bus would be ambushed as it drove throughout the streets was a fear that seemed all too promising. Plus the fact that the motorcade had bypassed the military airport for departure and was following a course to the further away civilian airport seemed even more mysterious. The implications of this unexpected route left me to wonder if they were planning to kill us. When we finally came upon the airport, it was closed. The lights from the bus pierced the darkness and the whispers from other passengers were the only sounds heard. We were flagged on through numerous security roadblocks. Directions of the next steps were passed from passenger to passenger as if not to awaken the sleeping citizens of Tehran: "Get off the bus quickly, pick up your luggage from the pile, and wait on the tarmac."

We rode directly onto the tarmac and met several other motorcades. Dozens of Americans from areas all over Tehran met in this single juncture where we were led to line up. Immediately before us, the moving staircase was pushed into place outside the door of the Pan Am plane. The baby blue circular sign on the fuselage caught my attention. The first and last time I saw it was when I was pregnant and on my way to prepare for having Yvonne. It was unbelievable to see how everything had since unfolded.

Here on the tarmac, at the end of my world, the world didn't end. I had the odd sensation, as I stood silently waiting to board, that Iran, my country and home, was about to be a permanent memory left in my heart. All the things I took for granted unknowingly that made up the day-to-day landscape of my existence: the gardens, my grandfather's swing, to hearing the call for prayer to the beautiful mountains were all about to fade from my life. A few steps before completely boarding the plane, the early morning breeze blew harder and the air smelled of peace as if inviting me to reconsider. It all came to me as I boarded.

"No, Curtis. I can't do this."

He nudged me and nodded for me to move along into the plane. "At this point, you don't have a choice. Your life will be in danger."

It was as if I was moved forward by a force beyond my control. Once inside, the whole plane sat strangely silent. The air was thick as we all waited in painstaking anticipation of the takeoff. Then, the pilot announced the beginning of the flight. His Southern accent reminded me of Carter and then I fretted over the Shah's whereabouts all over again. The pilot directed us to focus our attention on the flight attendants who were preparing to demonstrate the regular safety drill before taking off.

There was a strong sense of proceeding as business as usual which only created more uncertainty in me. At any minute, I feared an explosion would cease the silence. I looked around at other passengers and saw they were equally scared by how their eyes were closed in prayer. Some had their eyes opened as if anticipating the worst at any moment. My eyes met another Iranian wife; it was like we were in solidarity with the same fear that since the plane hadn't taken off, it could still be captured or eventually shot down by a fighter jet. I heard the sound of the plane preparing for take-off. Every crank, click, and zoom of the engine magnified in my ears and my heart beat faster. I glanced from Yvonne and became fixated on Curtis' profile. For one brief moment, I could've sworn his features seemed almost demonic. His overbearing brow and jutting jaw made me shudder. All at once, I was flooded with every pain I experienced in America.

When the plane finally took off and was increasing altitude, my fears only magnified. At any moment the plane was going to be shot down. I held Yvonne tight, squeezing my eyes shut-my stomach, one giant knot. It felt like I was holding my breath for an hour. And then, like the voice of Allah, we heard the pilot announce, "We've just left Iranian airspace."

I could hear the pressure release from his voice when he spoke.

"Please be sure to thank the flight attendants who volunteered their service to make this mission possible. We will arrive in Switzerland shortly."

The entire plane broke out in applause and many burst into tears except for Curtis. I wondered why he was sweating. It was cold on the airplane. There was no reason for him to feel hot and I knew he wasn't afraid of flying.

"What's wrong Curtis?"

"That's it, Nusrat. We were on the last plane of Americans under the Pahlavi Dynasty to be evacuated."

Initially, I had a vague understanding of why things were unfolding as such, but now I was beginning to wonder how much was Curtis a part of making our arrangements to leave?

"If what you say is true, what's going to happen next?"

"I'm not sure. We have to wait and see."

I gave up and faced the inevitable truth of my situation. This was the way it had to be and things would improve. It was like what I had learned from American TV shows that portrayed the first few years of marriage as a struggle of acceptance and understanding. Since our marriage was still fresh, things would have a chance to improve. I always told myself, *No marriage was perfect and no two people were always in love.* I begged Allah to let his divine intervention come over Mrs. Brown. Maybe she could fall, break her hip, and enter a permanent coma? Not death, just a coma, so she wouldn't be a problem. What was I thinking? *Oh Allah, forgive my horrible thoughts.*

Yvonne cried from the turbulence, so I rocked her from side to side. I studied her tears trickling down both sides of her face. *Yes, it was the only thing to do.* If I had stayed in Iran, people would eventually figure out she was American (especially with the last name Brown). I thought to change her name to something more Iranian, but it would've complicated matters. In any event, it didn't matter now. We were on the plane and Yvonne would have a chance at a better future.

This was my destiny I concluded. My attempts of escaping my husband had ended. I saw beyond his words in that there was something else, but I couldn't put my finger on it. If I knew the worst was yet to come, I never would have left my country.

During our layover in Switzerland, we learned the Shah lost power to Ayatollah Khomeini. This news amplified my current mental state leaving me more overwhelmed with so many forces out of my control. I had no idea what this meant for my family in Iran or if it would be possible for me to ever return. Given the atmosphere of corruption that pervaded Iran and now the last monarch in exile, I had to focus on positive aspects or risk losing my mind. For me, the U.S. had to represent fruitful possibilities. The power hub of the world was sure to allow me a position to advance in a career, give Yvonne the opportunity to have a better life, and finally put my mind to rest. Worrying about my daughter being killed over her American citizenship was now a thing of the past.

PART TWO

Not a speck of sand, empty like a desert, my mother's soul. With a cargo of cedar wood and frankincense, a camel leaves a mosque and minaret dreaming of rain. A sandstorm is ahead. Praying for protection.

CHAPTER ELEVEN

We arrived in the U.S. on a frigid February morning and caught a taxi from Dulles airport to Mrs. Brown's home. When we passed the Washington Adventist Hospital, I knew we were close. Curtis mentioned he was interested in knowing whether the anticipated train station was up and running. Instead of just asking the cab driver about it, Curtis instructed him to drive down Cedar Street to see if it had opened. I wanted to go straight to his mother's house, but I kept my mouth quiet. Shortly, we drove past the station. It was running. We saw people walking about and waiting for various buses. Exhausted from traveling, I curbed my enthusiasm. *Could this mean I had a way to get around and enjoy a little freedom?*

"I didn't show you this side of Takoma Park before because this is the dangerous side closer to DC. Now with this station here, it's going to bring more problems and riff-raff."

Here he was talking to me like everything was normal when it wasn't. Though difficult, my silence meant peace for us all. When we got to the house, Curtis searched for the key. I stood next to him as a tightness came over my chest. It was like I couldn't breathe. I wanted to cry, but couldn't bring myself to do it. Then a sudden warmth came to my hand.

Yvonne had wet herself. "Curtis please hurry up and open the door. The baby had an accident."

As he was about to put the key in, the door opened. His mother stood before us. I had no idea what to expect.

"So you decided to bring the *nigger* back home?"

Instead of waiting for what else was going to come out her mouth, I ignored her and carried Yvonne through the door. Then I turned around just in time to catch Curtis pointing his finger between his mother's eyebrows, "Put a lid on it! I'm not in the mood for your crap!"

She pushed his hands out of her face. Unmoved by his behavior and more concerned with me making a mess she said, "I have the cloths lined up on top of the dresser."

I was already on the other side of the apartment when I heard her yelling from the front door, "Be sure to use the sabby on her bottom!"

Entering Curtis' room, I was overtaken by the dark memories of my pregnancy. I shut the bedroom door, put Yvonne on the bed, and focused on changing her diaper.

"Lie down, pretty baby. Don't cry, this will only be a minute." I consoled her with kisses and when I was done cleaning her up, I played with her feet by counting each toe. "One, two, three." Filled with delight by how her little feet squirmed, I tickled her a little more. "Four, five, and six!" I bent down and kissed the baby toe. She giggled and rubbed her eyes, my cue to pick her up and rock her to sleep. Then the clanking sound of Mrs. Brown's walker drew near. *She's probably going to tell me how to change her diaper as if I don't know how to do it already.*

She entered the room and looked around as if searching for a reason to argue. "How old is she now? She looks like she's two."

I put Yvonne in the middle of the bed and covered her with a blanket. "Mrs. Brown, she's twenty-one months old," I whispered, "and she just fell asleep, I need to get my bags out of the car."

She nodded her head, but I was still suspicious. Acting like she didn't hear me, Mrs. Brown nearly pushed me out the way with her walker. Heading out of the room, I overheard her mumbling, "This is my damn house and if I want to talk loud, I will. She can't tell me what to do in my home."

I waited at the door relying on my ear to determine what she was going to do next. I heard her again, "I haven't seen my grandbaby for a whole damned year."

Making sure she wouldn't see me, I stole a glance to see what she was doing. I observed her peeping over the bed. She looked at Yvonne as if she was dissecting her every feature.

"Damn it if she doesn't look just like her mother! *Just like her!* This baby doesn't have one thing from us Browns. Not a thing. She doesn't have our hair," she touched Yvonne's full head of black tresses. "Our eyes," she grazed the baby's forehead with her finger from one side to the other. "Nor our mouth." Cupping the small foot, it was as if she realized the biggest difference of all, "and these feet. Dear Lord, you know these feet." She closed her eyes and said, "these feet here are *nigger* feet."

How on earth did I find myself in such a family? Instead of loving Yvonne, she had distinguished the baby's physical attributes from her own. What was wrong with her? *Oh Allah, please give me the strength to ignore this woman. Please bring your divine intervention to get Yvonne and me out of this situation, far away from this evil.*

⊸⧽⊱ ⊰⧼⊶

To avoid our documents from being compromised or declared invalid due to the strained relationship between Iran and America, we married again in Rockville, Maryland on June 3, 1979. Standing before the Justice of Peace in an office to sign papers, I remembered how this was nothing like my wedding day in Iran. From the altar in my cousin's backyard, I saw the beautiful wedding sofreh and my reflection in the mirror set on the lavish spread. *Finally, I was marrying Curtis, a man Allah had chosen for me.* I gazed at the audience through my veil. Then, the music played and my love appeared. When his eyes first caught sight of me, I saw how he beamed with pride. In front of my entire family and guests he declared, "My God Nusrat, you look like an angel from heaven."

Two years later, I was signing a marriage contract with a toddler in my arms and no family in sight. This was far from romantic, but necessary, so I did it. As I expected, his mother didn't attend our civil ceremony. It would've been a nice gesture seeing that she missed our wedding in Iran. Unlike before, it was clear that she was against us being together. Understanding her position as a loud defender of race purification, I saw how, in her eyes, I had ruined her bloodline.

It didn't make sense. Why would Curtis marry me knowing his mother would disapprove? In Iran, he never mentioned any of this. How did he expect us to live in peace like this? When I talked with him, he shrugged it off, "My mother wouldn't like anyone I was with. That's just the way she is and she isn't going to change. Why don't you just get it?"

How was I supposed to get it? I thought my husband adored me enough to protect me from harm's way. All that I've worked hard for in my life was reduced to his mother's racist beliefs: anything non-white, non-American was horrible and insignificant. Instead of being an Iranian, I was now a "colored" woman, a "foreigner." No matter how hard I tried, I couldn't wrap my brain around my husband's motives.

Always looking for a logical response, I brought this issue up on several occasions until he finally said, "Why does all this matter to you? Your job is to stay at home and take care of your family. Don't let yourself get distracted from that."

"Distracted? I was somebody in my country and now I'm just what you and your mother say. Didn't you know I was *not* American when you were in *my* country? You know I'm Iranian, don't you? Curtis, you know the history of Iran." I felt my chest tighten. "And you know it's the land of the Aryans. We've discussed this long ago."

"That's not the point." His temper boiled over. "What happened to the wife I married in Iran? Did you think I forgot about you running from me at the consulate? Now you're bundled in the same goddamned category as everyone else."

"So you agree with your mother? If I was so low and disgusting, why would you marry me a second time? And I recall in Iran, we were equals. Remember how competent I was? Remember my awards?"

What went wrong? Why did my husband change from a charming man to a monster? I knew, and yet I didn't know. Was he delusional? I remembered his behavior in the past three years. I couldn't foresee the political events shaping his behavior against me or Yvonne. Was that why he changed? Or was this in him the whole time? Was he blinded to the societal problems he could face? Did he believe his mother was the voice of society? Did other Americans see him as "going outside of his own kind?"

⚬

It wasn't long before things went from bad to worse. The weatherman had reported a record-breaking Saturday in July with the temperature hitting one hundred degrees. I finished washing Yvonne's clothes and had pinned them on the line to dry in the backyard. When I returned to the house, I found her sitting alone in the living room playing with blocks. I searched the apartment for Curtis or his mother to find out why they left her unattended. Entering the kitchen, I couldn't believe what my eyes saw: Curtis punched his mother in the face and knocked her down to the floor.

There were times when I had witnessed my parents argue, maybe even shove each other a little, but that was the extent of their aggression. Their problems often played out in minor fits or temper tantrums. Never did things escalate into anything like this. His mother appeared unconscious. "What's wrong with you? She's not moving and blood is coming from her nose! You killed her!"

"I killed her?" He put his hand in front of her nose to see if she was breathing. "It's going to take more than that to put this blood sucking bitch out of her misery."

"*What?* How could you talk like this? What's *wrong* with you?" I didn't understand what was happening. "You heartless son of a bitch!" I pushed him against the wall. "How could you? What am I supposed to do if you go to jail?" Pounding my fists upon his chest, I abandoned all fear that he would hit me back. "This is *not* the *life* I came *here* to live!" I couldn't stop. "I did *not* come all the way *here* for this!"

"Watch it Nusrat," he flicked my hands away, "you're getting carried away now."

Behind me, on the floor came his mother's voice, "Why don't the two of you help me up?"

I rushed to her immediately, "Are you okay Mrs. Brown?"

"I'm fine. Just help me up and hand me the telephone."

I saw Curtis leave as if he was heading out of the house.

"Where are you going?"

"Nowhere. I'll be right back."

His mother called the police and Curtis was arrested. The next morning he got out. Though troubled by this event, I was glad there was now a wedge between him and his mother. Was this the answer to my prayers? Maybe now we could move on without her in the picture? In either measure, the task at hand was to find a place to live. I had to forget about the past and put myself into Curtis and Yvonne. How was I going to manage this all with my husband's ever-changing personality? Was he the man I married? Really, who was he?

It was hard for me to identify similar traits between us now. It was like everything changed once I no longer worked with my husband. I believed subconsciously the differences were what attracted me to him ultimately. Showing restraint from me was like an act of discipline. Neglecting to be warm and hospitable was how he avoided rejection. All the while, I thought he believed he was shrewd and wise. But the main difference that I was sure had set us apart was passion. For me, a life without it was stale. For someone like Curtis, too many feelings were considered overbearing and suffocating. Unless money and power were involved, these were something else.

He was prudent with his money. Together we had saved a total of eighty thousand dollars while living in Iran. His money came primarily from what he collected from his salary. My money came from what I kept while working before our marriage and from wedding gifts. After eight months of living with his mother, we found a home where a Hungarian couple lived and were preparing to retire and downsize. When we visited the property, I was charmed by the Faberge eggs that filled the apartment like a museum. With fancy beading and delicate hand-painted designs, the eggs were the good luck I needed. We signed the deed to our new home before a lawyer and a notary on September 23, 1979.

⇒⊹ ⊹⇐

A few miles away from his mother, our house sat on the corner of Garland Avenue. With three full apartments and one attic of which only Curtis and I could access, the place felt like home. The immediate location featured apartment rentals and landscaped areas with shrubs and holly bushes. The neighborhood had a steady flow of foreigners like me and was close to Columbia Union College.

Though things had been bumpy between us, I knew there was something in my husband that appreciated my desire for independence. When I told him we needed things, he always gave me the money without a problem. As the head of our household, he insisted on paying for half the house. I liked the idea that we were a team on this journey. Not only could this situation prove to be an excellent home for us, but also a smart investment. My parents helped us in furnishing our entire apartment. Maybe this was why Curtis gave in to my desire on having dark wood Colonial-style décor, but who knows?

Our apartment was in the middle and leveled to the street. And like the other two apartments, it had two bedrooms, one bathroom, a spacious living room, a modest dining area, and a kitchen. We chose to live in the middle apartment because the bottom apartment reminded Curtis of his childhood. I had also thought living in the middle was a smart way to gain insight into the lives of our renters by being under one floor and over the ceiling of the other. We were finding our way, making a life.

My husband insisted on collecting the rent payments and keeping up the property. My job was to take care of landlord duties while he was at work during the day. It seemed to me that I had assumed a similar role to the one his mother played when she raised her family with Louis. Except I was a pleasant landlord, making up for my husband's shortcomings as needed. We were set. The money from the rentals covered our mortgage and monthly expenses. I quickly grew confident in taking on the role of managing the tenants and creating relationships with neighbors. One in particular, Amy, was from Palestine and we kind of treasured any moment we could speak Arabic to one another. She told me that I reminded her of her sister back home. Every chance she got, she complimented me, "You're so pretty Nusrat. And I just love your clothes."

However, I believed she was the more attractive one since she was tall, thin, and didn't have a big stomach like me. I rarely found anything at the nearby Montgomery Ward, Woodies, or Peck and Beck to flatter my shape. Amy introduced me to a nearby Pakistani seamstress whose tailored clothing was reasonably priced. All I had to do was purchase the fabric, explain what design I wanted, and the seamstress designed the clothes beautifully. It was adorable how she designed matching outfits for Yvonne. I'd wear a low-cut shallow pump to give me a little height, put Mary Janes on the little one, and we were a sight. All of my clothes were made with matching scarves. I would easily loop it around my neck for easy access to cover my head if needed. Quite like my marriage, I had found a way to make things work.

Soon the quaintness of the area replaced my initial experience with Mrs. Brown. I was ready to start over and be the best possible wife and mother I could be. Practicing recipes from my Betty Crocker cookbook, I daydreamed of preparing my first Thanksgiving dinner in our new home. *The way to a man's heart was through his stomach*, I realized was true. Rarely did Curtis quarrel with food in his mouth.

I made a game where he tasted my American recipes and had to tell me what he thought. I prepared casseroles, pot roasts, and cakes. Sometimes he spoke of my improvements, but other times he compared my cooking to something his mother or a former girlfriend made better. "Well, I'm just being honest," he would say, and then I'd work extra hard at making it better. I came to learn that no matter what I did, I was no match to his past.

Nearly two months in our home, I thought it would be a nice idea to cheer things up a bit. I decided to throw a dinner party. The idea of people dancing, eating, and chatting inspired me. I invited Amy and some Iranian women I had met in the area who were also married to Americans. Hot tea was served to the guests, and when my husband entered the living room, he looked surprised at what I had put together. There were four couples already laughing and delighting in Yvonne, the only child present, dancing for them like a real performer. It was a Saturday night, husbands left their suits at home and wives wore their best heels and dresses. And with the flickering of the tapered candles on the mantle of the fireplace, each face beamed in the warm evening light. Serving tea cookies to a couple, I noticed Curtis mingling with others. I was pleased by this sight as he knew no one. I invited them all for a gathering to celebrate an occasion that not one of them knew about: my husband's birthday. It was all so lovely. It uplifted me to see him happy and making new friends. One, in particular, Lili, had a black husband, which made Curtis uneasy at first. He said, "I don't want Yvonne around them too much. I don't want her thinking it's normal."

It was strange how my husband quickly changed when he learned Lili's husband was also in Vietnam. Where did he really stand on race?

On November 4, 1979, the Iran Hostage Crisis happened. This event was sure to change the relationship between Iran and America forever. From my television set, I saw it all: the blindfolded hostages, the students waving red, white, and green flags screaming "Death to America!" The familiar images of burning tires in the streets and mass demonstrations broke my already shattered heart. So far away from who I was in my country, I feared now more than ever that I would never be able to return. I constantly monitored the extreme thoughts of despair taking over my mind.

Everything I had experienced up until this moment refined my political awareness. I was sure the Revolution would negatively affect women, I just didn't know how devastating it was going to be long-term.

The havoc taking place in Iran confirmed that I had ultimately made the right decision to come to America. New religious laws and policies resulted in many Iranian women migrating to other countries, an act I already carried through. Oppressed by Sharia laws, Iranian women now lost several rights that they had previously achieved. Once upon a time, we were more advanced than many parts of the world. Now, everything was one tragedy after another. I kept my feelings to myself and feared for the safety of my parents. One thing was for sure, Khomeini could make women cover, but he couldn't take their minds.

But, as much as I tried to hide behind my clothes, I knew my wit and intelligence never went unnoticed by Curtis. I guess one could say he didn't expect me to take up an interest in politics and journal writing. My attempts at including him failed. Once I asked him how he thought it was best to address the president in a letter I had written. I wondered if it was more appropriate to address President Ronald Reagan as *In the name of the All Mighty God, Leader of Our World, The President of the United States Ronald Reagan* or just *Dear President Ronald Reagan?*

"It doesn't matter. No one's going to read your goddamned letters anyway."

With the U.S/Iran relationship heavily strained, I stayed updated on the news by reading the Washington Post and watching television. Curtis would tell me to "cut that crap off!"

God forbid if he found my writing, he would probably explode. He only wanted me focused on taking care of Yvonne, the house, and the tenants. Anything else was off limits. In my journal, I jotted down notes for letters I would later write to various officials including my latest interest in Beverly LaHaye, a Christian conservative activist who founded *Concerned Women for America*. LaHaye had a lot to say lately about pro-family issues. Quite like me, she took issue with Gloria Steinem and Betty Friedan who were the voice on women's liberation. Despite our different religions, I was pleased we saw eye to eye on daycare. I wrote to her as soon as I could.

Re: Television Program "Working Mothers on 20/20"

Dear Beverly LaHaye,

I saw the program that focused on the average American family where the husband and wife work to pay their expenses such as a mortgage or rent. At the end of the show, Barbara Walters mentioned how difficult it was to be a working mother. She acknowledged the difficulties posed on the working mother stuck in a lousy marriage and suggested there were better days ahead. Here are some points that I would like to share with you:

- Being a mother is not a part-time job.
- Motherhood is a lifetime job-once it starts it never ends.
- Children are better raised and nourished from their mother at home than in a daycare center.

In the early stages of life, the child needs stability. Feeding, nursing, bathing, changing clothes, hugging, holding, talking to, and of course love are all critical aspects of molding a child for success. If the child becomes sick, it's the mother's responsibility. Assisting the child with physical muscle development like holding the child's hand and helping him or her to walk are an important aspect to their lives and are best to take place in the home.

Even with all the best daycare regulation, I do not believe it is possible for a group of children to receive the same tender care that would come from home with their own mother. I thank you for taking the time to read my letter and welcome a response if you so choose.

Sincerely,
Nusrat Brown

Then the day came where he finally read one of my letters. His reactions to my thoughts annoyed me. He said things like "Who do you think you are? Do you think anyone cares what you have to say? You're just a pretty face."

It was like his remorse for marrying me grew stronger with every attempt on my part to voice my opinion. Did he really believe what he said? Was I really just a *pretty face*? Did he forget my education and the value my parents had put on books? Why would this surprise him? It seemed my *pretty face* now triggered his inadequacies which only made him ferociously jealous.

"Go to Peck and Beck and pick yourself some new dresses. You're in America now." He pulled out a women's catalog that sat in the pile of junk mail. "See these women? They're nice looking. I'm not saying I don't appreciate how you look, but get yourself some nice things to wear."

Initially, I thought he said this to me because he cared about our image as a family. But it felt like he was just trying to control me.

"You have the potential to be a great American wife." He pinched my cheek, "Which is why I married you, not once but *twice*."

"Oh, thanks. You know I'm doing my best. And I thought you should know I'm thinking about cutting my hair."

"What do you mean?"

"It's difficult to manage my hair, take care of Yvonne, and keep up with the house."

"You already know how I feel about that. We don't need to discuss this any further. If you cut your hair, I'll cut you."

"Seriously?"

"Of course not. Just don't do it.

CHAPTER TWELVE

The date was January 20, 1981. I changed the television set back and forth between the morning shows until I watched President Ronald Reagan being sworn in. Two years earlier we were on the last plane of Americans leaving Iran and now the hostages were released after 344 days. I had seen Reagan with his perfect dark hair speak sincere hope. With tears in my eyes, I thought it was finally possible that the U.S. and Iran could reconcile their relationship.

I blanked it out of my mind that Curtis had ever hit me or that things were ever rocky. I now lived in a new country-new home-new life and things were going well. Starting over with a clean slate meant things were sure to be different. However, I didn't understand the depth of Curtis' insecurities until he took me to the doctor for a follow-up appointment to check my thyroid.

In the past two months, I had noticed an unexplained weight gain and felt too hot to wear a jacket in chilly February weather. I attributed it all to my underactive thyroid. Busy with multi-tasking the home and family, I hadn't refilled my prescription in three months and believed the effects had finally caught up with me. Amy watched Yvonne so that

Curtis could accompany me to the doctor's office. For me, it was like visiting an all-too-familiar place. But with Ali posted at his security desk, I broke into a happy smile.

"Welcome back, Nusrat!"

"Good to see you, Ali!" I turned to introduce Curtis to Ali when I saw the immediate red flames on Curtis' face. "This is my husband."

"Nice to meet you, sir."

Ali had to have sensed the tension, but made it worse by adding, "You have a lovely wife."

Immediately, I turned to watch Curtis' reaction. Swelling with fear, I saw how he nodded reluctantly in agreement. It was clear to me that he was angry by the way his face strained to stay composed. He didn't say anything and took a seat in the waiting room. To avoid public humiliation, I put my head down and walked quickly to the doctor's office.

Sitting on the examination table, I heard the protective paper crunch under my thighs. The smell of clean, unopened rubber gloves lingered faintly in the room. Dr. Goodway entered with my medical record in hand. "Good morning, Mrs. Brown." He sat on his round swivel chair facing in my direction. "How are you feeling today?"

"I think my thyroid is acting up." I massaged my throat area. "I'm tired and I'm experiencing unexplained weight gain."

"I see." He began his examination and then reached for his stethoscope and placed it on my back. He listened and moved it around slowly and then stopped at my lower back. "This bruise on your back, does it hurt?" He lightly touched the area, "It's the size of my hand."

"Oh, it's nothing. I bumped into something." I composed my face. "I bruise easily, Dr. Goodway. By any chance, did you get my test results yet?"

"Are you sure? If I didn't know any better, I would say it was in the shape of a footprint."

"A footprint?"

"Is there something you want to talk about?"

I sat in shock. I didn't know how to respond. As if he perceived my resistance, the doctor reassured me of patient confidentiality.

"I have a daughter to raise Dr. Goodway and she deserves to be raised by a mother *and* a father. Please understand my position."

"Very well." He picked up my medical folder. "Then I guess I shall congratulate your daughter?"

"What do you mean?"

"Mrs. Brown, your thyroid is not the issue. Given your weight gain and your family medical history, I am afraid you are at risk for gestational diabetes mellitus."

The only word I heard the doctor say was "diabetes."

"I have *diabetes*? Like my mother?"

"No. You have a temporary case that can potentially be permanent if you do not watch your carbohydrate consumption."

"I don't understand doctor."

"Mrs. Brown, you are pregnant. And from my examination, I estimate you to be twelve weeks along with a due date of September 15, 1981."

To say I was shocked would have been an understatement. Pregnancy was farthest from my mind. My period wasn't late and intercourse was infrequent. What God would permit me to carry another child? Yvonne was now four, walking and talking, potty trained, and would be in kindergarten soon. She was sweet, making it easy to manage and love. But what if this baby turned out like Curtis making my life unbearable? What if this baby was also born with twelve toes? I would have to endure more of his disappointment and bear the stress again of facing surgery to remove the extra digits. The doctors said Yvonne would have surgery once she turned five and now this was going to happen with another baby in the picture? I didn't want it. And to think this pregnancy was already complicated by diabetes, a disease that was killing my mother. The devastation this brought to an already terrible situation was nothing short of complicated.

Making my way to the waiting room to meet Curtis, I decided to keep the pregnancy a secret. As we exited the building, I avoided Ali's eyes and walked out the door several steps behind my husband. I did a visual check-in of Curtis' facial expression and body language to assess his current state. Had he calmed down? Was he over his jealousy? Was he concerned about my health? Or was he ready to fight? Gauging his ferocity and accepting the baby in my womb was too much. Sitting in the car, I chose silence, hoping it would automatically smooth over any issues he may have been experiencing. He drove for ten minutes in complete silence until he finally spoke.

"So, do you want him?"

"What are you talking about? Want *who?*"

"He's from your country, isn't he? How does he know I have a *wonderful wife?* What went on between you two? And to think I was working hard for you in Iran?"

"Are you crazy? You are *my* husband. Why are you accusing me of this? All I do is stay home, cook, and clean. I take care of my family and here you are with this?"

"I saw how he looked at you. I saw you smile at him."

"The security guard always saw me by myself while I was pregnant. I haven't seen him since then. Maybe he doesn't remember me having a husband because you weren't with me?"

I delighted in the jab.

When we got home, he asked me to go to the house before I picked Yvonne up from the next door neighbor. It wasn't clear to me what he was thinking so I just sat in the living room while I heard him in the kitchen opening and shutting drawers. Then I got the idea to go to the bedroom and examine the bruise on my back. As I passed the dining room, I caught Curtis setting a hammer on the table. He stopped me and said, "Hand me your ring."

"Why?"

"If you don't give it to me, I'm going to snatch it off myself."

I gave it to him and followed him to the dining room. He placed the ring on the table next to the hammer. I watched as he grasped the handle of the hammer and gritted his teeth. He then smashed the ring into pieces. Gathering the pieces in his palm, he held it up to my face and said, "Now you, 'Ms. Lovely woman' are no longer married and now Ali can see you as a single woman without a husband."

After blowing the ring remnants in my face, he threw the hammer out the back window. I was positive that it had landed in Amy's front yard.

"But *you're* my husband!" I wailed, "and I'm *pregnant!*"

And then it was as if dark clouds parted in the sky after a hurricane and the sun came out beaming over the land, creating a sudden joy washing over Curtis' face.

"A baby?" He said.

His voice went from harsh and sharp to soft and lullaby sweet.

"Nusrat!"

He fell to the floor and kissed my bare feet.

"Please forgive me-I didn't know-I had no idea."

So filled with regret and remorse at carrying, birthing, and taking care of another child, I sobbed. I lost all hope for my life and the child in my womb. He clung to my leg pleading, "Please forgive me…I didn't know." He stood up and hugged me tightly, "I love you. I love Yvonne. I love our baby." He gently placed his palm over my stomach. "I know I'm not the best man in the world. I know I've made a lot of mistakes. But, so help me God, I'm going to buy you another ring. I'm going to be there for you, more than I've ever been before. I promise."

As much as I wanted to believe what he said, his dark side scared me more than anything. I'm not sure if it was possible for him to become a decent human being. And to think I was dedicated to keeping a promise of Yvonne being born in America. He wanted an American child to trap me, not so she could have better opportunities. With our daughter, he knew he had me where he wanted: in a dreadful position and pregnant again.

"Look at the table," I cried. "There's a big mark on it."

"Don't worry about that either, I'll take care of it. It's nothing, I'll sand it down to be good as new, I promise."

The next day when he went to work, I visited Amy. She asked me why my husband had thrown a hammer in her yard. My response came quick, "You know how men are when it comes to their tools. He didn't like the way the handle gripped. So he got rid of it. Please accept our apologies for it landing in your yard."

Curtis didn't approve of our friendship. He thought Amy "meddled in our business." But I knew this was just another play of control. He also believed she gave Yvonne poisonous candy. I assured him that his ideas were right and that I wouldn't dare let our daughter around her again. Keeping this from Amy, I was curious to know if she thought I had looked pregnant or if she noticed my empty ring finger. If she did, she said nothing.

Pulverizing my wedding ring was something I couldn't forget. For days, Curtis focused on controlling his temper. His new behavior helped me redirect my focus on Yvonne and the baby in my womb. Every now and again he permitted me to go to a Tupperware party, grocery store, or to the mosque. I was convinced we were on the mend. Sadly, I was wrong. A new habit formed: raising his hand as if to hit me "just in case I had a hard time knowing my place." One minute I could calm him down with expressions of love and seconds later he would snap all over again. If I didn't miscarry, it would be a miracle.

CHAPTER THIRTEEN

1981 and 1982 were years blurred by a consistent push and pull. By 1983, Yvonne was six. I had two more children: Darlene, age 2 and Kevin, just 15 months old. How could I bring myself to express to my family what was going on? All these years I had lied to myself, fulfilling my role as the stereotypical battered woman where my excuses ran as fluid as the Potomac River. I repeated the same story over and over again in my mind: *Things would get better because they had to. There was no perfect marriage or husband. It wouldn't always be this way.* And through it all, I believed everyone had a life like mine behind closed doors. With just a little more dedication, I could make my marriage work. Living without Curtis and raising my children as a single parent was a reality I couldn't bear.

Curtis' temperament was unpredictable. I didn't know how to gauge his moods. Was it possible I married a lunatic? With each abusive episode came a series of minor verbal assaults. I counted my blessings in that they never occurred in front of the children. Thankfully what happened on the way to the consulate was the worst experience yet. Then the police began coming to our home. The same thing happened every time: the officers would look at me like I was ugly. It was strange. I wasn't sure if they were aroused at the thought of my husband dominating me or what. Then they would apologize for disturbing Curtis explaining how they didn't understand why the neighbors had called. I knew they could see the bruises on my face, but it didn't matter. Curtis was in control.

I never mentioned any of this to my parents. For what? Distance and circumstance had killed any hope that they could help. Besides, it would be selfish with all that was happening back home.

Unlike my initial hope of having the best of both worlds, raising the children was all-consuming. My social life, however minimal revolved around Donahue, Yvonne's school activities, and Curtis' work schedule. We didn't go out to dinner or take family outings, or Sunday drives. We didn't go to the movies for a date night escape to the Flower Theatre or dinner at Ms. K's Toll House like other couples. I survived my life by keeping everything inside, putting Curtis and the children ahead of my own needs. Needs that were simple, like who to talk to when there was a minor problem with a tenant, someone to provide a ride to the pediatrician, or someone to give me reassurance that I was doing a reasonable job juggling all my responsibilities with three children.

To top it all off, I suspected he was cheating. His recent change in work hours to the graveyard shift was a spark for speculation and he had stopped touching me. Nothing was as consistent as the plaguing ache that struck my chest when I most wanted his tender embrace. Yesterday he complimented me on how beautiful and long my hair was growing. While the attention was nice, I couldn't fight off the desire to chop it all off. With a new-found confidence, I prepared to go to the hairdresser the next morning. Just as I was on my way, I received a phone call from my father. It had been months since I had heard from him.

"Nusrat Joon?" I heard him say.

"Ello Baba! Ello?" I couldn't hear him on the phone. I figured there was a bad connection instead of a silent pause.

"She's gone Nusrat."

"What do you mean?"

"Your mother is dead."

The phone hit the floor and my wailing began. It was the darkest October of my life. Later my father would explain how she died from complications of diabetes, but I knew better. Maman died from a broken heart. Burdened by the distance because of my marriage and not watching her grandchildren grow up is what really did it. My mind produced images of my mother gasping or pushing out her last breath, her cold, unmoving frail hand without my hand to hold, the image of her asking to see Yvonne one last time, and the devastating reality that I would not be there. "We'll see you soon, Maman," I would say knowing otherwise.

It was too much for me to take in. Now I had to go to Iran for Maman's funeral when I wasn't even able to make it while she was alive. How was that going to work? At this point, Curtis rejected the idea of me taking the children out the country.

Word spread around the mosque about my mother's death. One generous Sister offered to lend me money to travel with the children. After seriously considering it, I had to decline. How could I manage three children in an airport, much less on a ten-hour flight? Going to the grocery store with them was exhausting enough. The thought of such a task had made me put it off until we were down to the last piece of bread and cheese. Walking twelve blocks to the store with an umbrella stroller while holding hands with the kids, and then the shopping, and finally carrying the groceries all the way back home was stressful. Not to mention the difficulty of walking against traffic and protecting the children from getting hit by a car. And, what about last week when I ran into a women's lib representative? From the front of the grocery store, she stood shouting at me. "Woman, make up your mind and join our organization!"

Who the hell was this woman to talk to me like this? What kind of group discouraged women from the home and insisted they work? How dare she recruit at the grocery store.

"Liberate yourself and join the Feminist Movement."

"Thank you, but I know my position in life. I have three children, a husband and I'm a housewife. I have one baby nursing, one on a bottle, and a little girl. All of them deserve the care of a mother."

By the look of her irritated face, it was clear she didn't expect that response from me, but it was true.

"That's fine. Suit yourself, but what about *you?*"

"I'm fine."

No, I couldn't pull it off. I concluded it was impossible for me to travel. The thought of grieving over my mother's grave while the children ran around the place made my head hurt. It just wouldn't work. Besides, there was no way I could repay the money and Curtis wouldn't dare contribute a penny.

It was all so painful. I cried for my mother, for myself, and for what felt like a lethal dose of regret. I knew the day would eventually come when my parents would die, but I never imagined it happening as it did. Should I have left my country? But what would have happened to Yvonne? And then, like a loudspeaker in my mind, came the words of Hayedeh, the famous Iranian singer that I still couldn't believe I had met in person at the consulate, "Be strong my crying girl, freedom is a rose petal many died for."

It was like a verse in a song, a line from a poem solely inspired by the bruises and clear evidence of defeat written all over my face. Was this single isolated incident supposed to be something I clung to in moments of despair? It amazed me how the words popped into my mind out of nowhere.

I settled for having a memorial service at the mosque for Maman. I had believed, despite my ignorance and naïveté, that choosing to come to America would benefit Yvonne. Now I realized it hadn't served me well in any way. At least I had my family and a home. There was one thing that Curtis and I could agree upon: the children needed to be raised in the home by me, their mother. All of this was my life now, a vast sea of regret. More change would come when I learned Curtis, my husband of 5 years, was capable of shooting me dead.

CHAPTER FOURTEEN

It was a Friday morning in June 1983 and I was preparing to go to the mosque. Carefully removing my rollers, I brushed out the curls to get a full bounce. My thinking was to make myself up hoping to feel better on the inside. My appearance was one of the few things I could control, so I decided to change things up. Dressing like I did when I was a working woman, I put on my black and white herringbone-tweed cape jacket-suit and a string of pearls. I knew it was drastic, but I needed a change. I did my makeup, sprayed some perfume, and was prepared for the day.

Curtis' behavior that morning hadn't been at all menacing before I went to the mosque for Jummah, Friday prayer. Preferring to spend time with the kids on Fridays, he adjusted his work schedule to lighten my burden. He was finally coming around and becoming a bit of a partner again. This morning was a typical Friday where he prepared breakfast, watched cartoons with the children, and then returned to bed while I got everyone ready. Leaving the house, I had no sense of any impending danger. On the way to the babysitter's house, I remembered Yvonne had a check-up appointment. I turned around and headed toward the pediatrician's office before I made it to the mosque. As a result, we returned home half an hour later than what I initially told Curtis.

Upon entering the house, the girls darted to their room to play, and I placed the baby in the bouncer. I expected him to be resting since he had to be at work by 8:00 pm.

"Curtis, we're home," I said from the front door so he could have time to get appropriate. "Can you keep an eye on the children while I cook?"

"What's that smell?" He asked as I entered the bedroom to change my clothes.

"I'm not sure. Do you think something is burning?"

"It's so strong that it woke me up."

"Oh, I hope it's not my perfume. I didn't think I sprayed much. I'm so sorry."

"Isn't that what I got you for Mother's day last year? What's today's date?"

"June 20, 1983."

"It's not a holiday is it?"

"It's not. I can wipe it off if you like."

"No. That's not the point. Why are you wearing it? Who do you want to smell good for? Where did you say you went today? The mosque? Like that?"

"You know I went to the mosque. I forgot Yvonne had a check-up appointment today. Instead of going to the babysitter, I took her to the doctor's before I went to the mosque. Then I came straight home."

"Looking like that? Smelling like that?"

"What's wrong Curtis? You don't like it? I wished you'd come to the mosque with me, but you don't. All I did was take her to the pediatrician and pray."

"Why didn't you take the kids with you?"

"Did you hear what I just said? I did, and besides, I'm with them every day, all day. Don't I deserve some time to myself?"

Removing the sheet from his body, he grabbed for something off the side of the bed. Facing the mirror with my back to him, I briefly combed my hair. Wearing only his underpants, he walked up behind me. I turned around, meeting a gun aimed at my heart. I was sure he was crazier than usual in his eerily calm and demented mental state.

"Where were you?"

Where did the gun come from? I didn't know he had a gun. Although shocked, I understood this wasn't the time to show any sign of fear. He put it on my heart. Instinctively, I leaned forward and felt the barrel of the gun. With a slight pull on the trigger, I knew my life could end at any second. I met his calm stance with an equally cool posture. Neither of us had seen that in me before. "Don't be stupid," I said as I moved past him nonchalantly like dinner was the next important event. Everything happened so fast. From behind, he grabbed me by the collar, and we wrestled until he slapped me with his free hand.

"You're going to get the hell out of this house, you little whore!"

"I'm not going anywhere!" I insisted, but he walked me out the bedroom to the front door where he opened it and kicked me from behind. Landing on my face, I felt the burn on my cheeks from scraping the concrete.

I got up and sat on the bench by the front door. I prayed the children remained in the house not realizing what had happened. Yvonne was hopefully occupied with her dolls, Darlene was still napping, and Kevin was playing in the crib. I couldn't imagine the children seeing what their father had done. I tried to enter the house but it was locked, so I sat back down. The midafternoon sun beamed on my face and the heat was growing unbearable. Looking back, I saw Curtis from the window. I lost it.

"You said you'd be there for me! You said you loved me and that you were sorry! What does this all mean?" I screamed until my throat hurt and defeat consumed me. "I've learned my lesson. You can let me back in Curtis."

I heard the sound of him unlocking the door and finally, it cracked open. I couldn't bring myself to look in his direction.

"The kids are crying. They need their mother."

Immediately I got up to see what was wrong. *Curtis was sure to never take his anger out on the kids, right?* To prove I wanted peace I assured him by begging him to forgive me.

"I'll never leave the house again. I promise."

I only got as far as the storm door when he punched me in the mouth with his fist. It was after this that he allowed me back in. I checked the children for any signs of redness or bruises. Besides their cries, they were fine. From the corner of my eye, I saw him go into the bedroom. "Don't let the kids bother me," he cautioned. From the bed, he added, "It would serve you well to put them to sleep and take care of your wifely duties before I leave for work tonight."

Finally, something clicked in my mind: if my husband could put a gun to my heart, then he would try again to kill me. I dressed the kids and waited for him to go to sleep. I took them immediately to Amy's house. My plan was to steal away for a moment long enough to call the police. There was no time for me to clean up my face, worry about scarring, or what the neighbors would think. It was not until I saw the fear in my children's eyes from looking at my face that I grew concerned. By now, my eyes were swollen and red. My nose, covered in blood, my mascara, smeared all around my eyes, and my cheeks were scraped on both sides. I assured the children that I was fine, "Don't worry, Mommy is okay. Why don't we go now to visit Amy?"

We didn't get far before I noticed the downstairs tenant walking towards me from their apartment. "Are you okay, Mrs. Brown?"

Before this moment, I believed people were clueless to my shame. Turning my head in the opposite direction, I kept walking. Once we got to Amy's, I called the police. I couldn't believe the words that came from my mouth: "Please help me! My husband put a gun to my heart threatening to kill me."

When they arrived, I feared Curtis' reaction would end in a blood-bath. Watching from the side of Amy's house, I saw the officers carry several rifles from out the house. At last, a handcuffed and half-naked Curtis was sent to jail. *Where did all the guns come from? How could he have all of them in the house with our children?* An officer instructed me on what to do next, "Go to the station and file charges against your husband. From there, you will be advised to take the kids somewhere safe. Do you have someone you can stay with?"

"No," I concluded.

Where else would I go? This was my home.

"Does anyone know where he got the guns from?"

"Not sure Ma'am. Your husband said something about the military, but it didn't make sense. We can take you to the Crisis Center. It sounds scary, but the women there are kind."

⇥⇤ ⇥⇤

Since the collapse of the Pahlavi Dynasty 5 years ago, my life spiraled downward at a supernatural speed. Curtis went to jail for beating up his mother, he tried to kill me, and now I was checking into a women's shelter. Asking God for an explanation proved to be a waste of time with every passing day.

Marrying Curtis didn't turn out to be like the fantasies I initially had about having a husband. I once saw myself living in a large pink marble castle entertaining family and guests on a daily basis while raising children and keeping up with cooking and house chores. My husband would be handsome, charming, and generous with praising his wife and mother of his children. I would wear elegant clothes and keep myself up, dividing my duties as mother and wife with ease. There would be lots of passion. When a disagreement arose, I imagined communication or sex would always solve the problem. No one would ever get hurt physically or emotionally. I would never be left to do it all by myself.

At first, the children sensed the excitement that was all about them in the crowded waiting room with other women and children. Praying the younger children were too young to understand what was happening, I was especially worried about Yvonne. Her 6-year-old eyes were all too familiar with seeing me abused by her father. Darlene and Kevin giggled, ran around, and climbed everywhere they could until Kevin fell asleep in a cardboard box in the waiting room. This would be an image I would never forget. In my heart, I knew all of this was affecting them somehow someway, but I didn't know how exactly. It was just too much.

Checking into the shelter was nothing short of humiliating. Presenting myself gracefully before Ms. Rose, the intake counselor was a mystery to me. How did I keep it together? Sitting in her office, Yvonne played with Darlene in earshot. Looking at my paperwork and then back at me, I could tell Ms. Rose noticed the condition of my face. I didn't think she expected someone who dressed like me to be this crushed.

"I like your suit, Mrs. Brown."

I didn't know what to say. The swelling and cuts on my face were something I couldn't cover up, no matter how put together I appeared.

"How did someone like you end up here?"

I recalled the entire incident as I had already done with the police. I also provided standard information relating to the date of birth, hair and eye color, and weight of me and the children. Some of the questions were unexpected, like "Why did you wait so long to tell anyone?"

"Because I keep my mouth shut. I was raised knowing that what happens in the house stays in the house."

"What do you want for your children?"

"I want my children to have a good education. I want them to be educated in a Catholic school or private school. I want my family to be under one roof."

"Catholic school? But you wrote on the form that you are Muslim."

"From kindergarten to fourth grade I attended a Catholic school in Bombay under the British rule."

"I see, Mrs. Brown."

Was she impressed or in disbelief? Instead of asking me another question, Ms. Rose jotted down some notes. Then she stated, "You're an intelligent woman, Mrs. Brown. But you need some street smarts about you."

Street smarts? This wasn't a quality anyone should have. It's for whores who work on the street.

"I'm here at the hands of an uneducated man and you want me to be 'street smart'? I'm not a 'street smart' kind of woman. My family, character, and upbringing do not condone your 'street smarts.' We were raised to be women of the home."

"Please forgive me. I didn't mean to offend you. It's just that men like this have patterns. If we know the signs, then we have street smarts. That's all I'm saying."

"I don't know anything about these signs. I don't know anything about dealing with the police or coming to a shelter. I don't know anything about this kind of life."

I saw past Ms. Rose's words and knew she was struggling to find a way to get through to me. Unable to resolve the cultural barrier, I knew this woman had difficulty identifying with my culture. It was as if she was trying to put me into an equation that didn't add up to her ideas of what a woman in this situation should look or act like. Licking her fingers to separate the pages, Ms. Rose pulled out the final sheet to go over.

"I need an inventory of your private belongings."

"I had just enough time to throw some clothes in a few trash bags. It's all I have."

"What about your purse?"

"My purse?" It was on my lap. What would she need with my purse?

"Yes, we have to document everything to make sure that all you came in with leaves with you."

I dumped the contents of my purse on her desk.

Are those bullets?" Ms. Rose picked up one. First, she examined it closely, then she looked back at me. "Why do you have three bullets in your purse, Mrs. Brown?"

"They are my husband's bullets. I found them in the house and took them. I'm sure he has more. But with these in my purse, I have three less worries of him killing me."

━━◄╼ ╾►━━

Living with other women and children who were also abused by the hands of a husband was agonizing. I prayed this short-term experience wasn't going to have long-term consequences on the children. With the help of the Crisis Center staff, I filed for a court order of protection from domestic violence. The court ordered the following: 1) I would get temporary custody of the children. 2) Spousal abuse was to stop. 3) My husband was to vacate the family home, and 4) a court date was set for Curtis to represent his side of the case.

While we were in the shelter for almost three weeks, Curtis refused to leave the house, which put him in contempt of court, a criminal offense. I didn't understand the rationale behind the current situation: he was court ordered to vacate the family home and refused to leave. Not only did this compromise our safety, but he was the reason we were at the Crisis Center in the first place. How could this make sense?

Our room was sterile and smelled like a hospital. How many women and children before us slept on the same bed as us wondering if this was all life had to offer? The walls like the floors were white and only one bathroom was shared by all the women and their children. We were expected to eat outside the shelter. Handing me some emergency money for food, Ms. Rose cautioned me, "There is a Safeway down the street. We advise women to eat from the salad bar to ensure they get nourishment during this difficult time."

So we ate fresh fruits and vegetables. The kids missed a hot-cooked meal just as much as I missed my kitchen. I could tell someone had attempted to make the room appear home-like by hanging up a painting of kittens. Besides the watermarks on the edges, I guess it was a nice touch. It stood there, hanging crooked on the wall above Yvonne's bed. If we didn't have the one window overlooking the parking lot, the place would have felt like a jail. To add to it all, there were no dressers which meant our belongings were in trash bags lined up on the floor.

As it was, we were safe, but far from the comforts of home and normalcy. At night, I rocked the younger children to sleep and watched Yvonne finally relax enough to rest. I felt terrible for our situation and all the women experiencing the same pain. I prayed for an escape from this reality for all of us. Before I went to sleep, I patted my left breast making sure I still felt my only twenty-dollar bill in my bra. Then I pulled out a notepad from one of the trash bags and sat on the bed. I didn't know where to begin. My thoughts were all over the place. With a little focus, I wrote the things that came to my mind most clear:

How did I end up here? How was I going to get through this? The children didn't deserve this life. I don't deserve this life. When will it all end? What did I do to deserve this from a man that vowed to love me? What am I going to say to the kids when they ask about their father?

It was midnight when I was about to go to sleep, but then Yvonne woke up crying from having a nightmare.

"Mommy, I can't get the dying boy out of my mind."

I didn't know what she meant at first, but then it came to me. Six months earlier we witnessed a boy hit by a car. Now, as I sat looking at her, the sound of a child crying and screaming from the next room unsettled my spirit. I'm sure this bothered her sleep.

"Are you okay Honey?"

"I think I'm okay. It's just another bad dream. What about you? Why are you still up?"

"Mommy is just writing. But let's try to go back to sleep."

On the day of the fateful accident, the school nurse called informing me how Yvonne had chicken pox and had to be picked up from school.

I drove Curtis' car to pick her up. On the way back home, we stopped at McDonald's. I locked all the doors and instructed Yvonne to stay in the car. Five minutes later, a fire engine and ambulance sprang out of nowhere. They parked just a few feet from my car. Leaving the bag of food at the register, I darted towards Yvonne. To my relief, she was still sitting quietly in the front seat. I opened the door, pulled her out, and hugged her tight.

"Mommy, what's wrong?"

I saw how she reached down scratching her legs.

"What happened over there?"

"I'm not sure."

A group of spectators surrounded the scene. Taking Yvonne by the hand, I said, "Let's go see what happened."

A lady dressed in a nurse's uniform had run over a child. Silently praying, I was unable to spare Yvonne's eyes from the scene: a round swirl of red and white spaghetti paint mixed together like an arts and crafts project gone wrong. Next to this was a white Converse shoe covered in tire marks. The other shoe was nowhere in sight. It belonged to its dying owner, a young boy. As flat as he was, I couldn't understand how he was able to still scream. The EMTs arrived and moved us from the scene. The nurse wailed over the body, now covered with a white sheet. Traumatized, we left immediately.

"Are you okay honey?"

"I hope that doesn't happen to me when I get older. I hope this doesn't happen to you, Mommy." Yvonne was full of bewilderment. "Why did he die? Is that going to happen to me?"

"To you?" I was surprised by her thinking. In Iran, death was more seen than hidden. The more one saw it as they grew up, the easier it was to accept. I figured it was a teachable moment for her to learn how death was also a big part of life. "Honey, we are all going to leave this earth, we just don't know when or how."

"But why did he get hit by the car?"

"He was crossing the street and didn't look both ways. Learn a lesson: always look both ways so that this doesn't happen to you," I advised.

"Let's talk about something else. How is your skin? Are you still scratching? Does it still itch?"

"It's still itching. But Mommy, am I going to die? Am I going to die like that?"

"No, that's not going to happen to you. I love you. Everything is going to be fine."

At 12:30 a.m., Yvonne was still haunted by the accident and I saw how this intensified her fear of our current situation in the shelter. Rubbing her back, I prayed she would return to sleep.

"I don't feel good, Mommy." She came to me and sat on the bed. "I can't sleep. The mother in the next room is still crying. She's loud. If daddy weren't so bad, we wouldn't be here. I miss my room."

"I know, Sweetie, I know. Don't worry. We will not be here forever. Now, go back to bed before we wake your brother and sister."

The next morning, a counselor knocked on the door and handed me a bag. "Your husband dropped this off for you and the children this morning."

Yvonne jumped out of her bed and ran toward me, "What's in it? What did daddy bring us?"

I pulled out a pack of juice, a bag of chips, and two letters. I handed a letter to Yvonne, "It's a note from your Grandfather. I'll read it to you in a minute." The other envelope, written in Curtis' handwriting, was addressed to "My Dearest Wife, Nusrat."

I ripped it open.

Dear Nusrat,

I'm worried sick about you and the kids. I'm working on getting you guys out of there as soon as possible. The house isn't the same without you and the children. I am dying for your love. Please find it in your heart to forgive me.

Your Loving Husband,
Curtis

My heart sunk to my stomach. *Could he have a change of heart? Would he make things better?* Folding the letter, I put it in my purse and felt a weight lifted. I saw Yvonne sitting in a chair next to the window waiting for me to read the letter from her grandfather. I walked to her, sat her on my lap and read:

Dearest Yvonne,

Salam Alaikum. It was so nice of you to remember your grandfather with a birthday card. I am doing fine and have no specific complaints except for my leg pain. However, I am glad to hear you are doing well. Remember to address me in writing as "Mr." for you should abide by the etiquette set by your elders. As my first grandchild, I love you deeply. I always pray for your success in life, especially in your studies. I kiss you and leave the rest to future writings. Write soon.

Affectionately yours,
Grandpa

Just as I was going to discuss how we would respond to his letter, the fire alarm went off in the shelter. Packing up the kids and our belongings, I prepared to evacuate the building. I saw this as a sign, an opportunity for us to return home. God made a way. Rushing the children down the stairwell, we were stopped by Ms. Rose.

"Don't worry, it's a false alarm."

"Oh my, are you serious?"

"It's okay." Ms. Rose smiled. "I'm actually glad I bumped into you. I want you to consider sharing your story to help other women. Like you, my husband threatened me with a gun. I wrote to Congress and they found it helpful to learn about this type of abuse."

I asked Yvonne to walk her brother and sister to the bus stop, then asked, "Ms. Rose, what do you mean help other women?"

Behind Ms. Rose was a bulletin board of missing women and children. Looking at their eyes, so filled with hope, broke my heart all over again. "How can I help other women? Look at me, I have three kids, my husband has problems, and you want *my* story? You should look for someone else."

Then the look I hated appeared, the eyes of pity.

"Are you sure that's what you want to do? He put a gun to your heart. What more evidence do you need this is not a safe situation?"

"He is genuinely sorry this time," I remembered his note. "He told me how miserable he is without his family. I've never heard him so remorseful. I can't live with myself knowing I gave up so easily on my marriage. I need to give it another try, at least for the sake of the kids. They deserve to have a family under one roof."

"If you insist, Mrs. Brown. I hate to say it, but I'm afraid it won't be long before you all return. Please take my card."

I took the card and stuffed it in my purse with the rest of my papers and junk, "Thank you. I have to go and look after my children." Walking away, I realized I had one more thing to say. "I appreciate all that you have done Ms. Rose. I just think my marriage deserves another chance."

"Very well Mrs. Brown. If you change your mind and want to make a difference in legislation, please call me at the number on the card." Praying to God for strength and direction, I made my way to the bus stop. I looked down at my fingernails in disgust. I had nothing, not even nails.

─═╪─ ─╪═─

Sweating, a camel carries a sign around her neck. It reads, "Never marry." Urine splashes and crystallizes down the legs. Projectile vomit for the enemy. How does one find beauty in the ugly?

CHAPTER FIFTEEN

After eighteen long days at the Crisis Center, we returned home on July 8, 1983. In this time, I grew a clearer understanding of my husband: he didn't indulge in drugs or alcohol which meant his problems could be worked out with time and care. Things were back to normal as much as they could be at this point. Pleasantly unexpected, I felt hopeful about our future as I observed some changes for the better: my husband was once again loving. He took us to the circus and purchased a Y membership for the children. I couldn't deny the burden it was for me to take them there, but it pleased me to see the children do something I couldn't do, swim.

Though strong-willed, Yvonne impressed me with how fair and accepting she was of her father. It was comforting to know she saw the same things I did. Her father wanted to work things out. Divorce wasn't a part of his plan. For a while, things were peaceful, but deep down inside I couldn't trust him as much as I wanted to. It was just a matter of time until another blow-up would occur. If I could get inside Curtis' head, then maybe I could foresee another incident and perhaps even prevent it from happening. So I took upon myself the role of a psychoanalyst like Dr. Freud, thinking this would be in our best interests.

It started with us talking more when Curtis came home from work. Sometimes we talked for hours, mostly about job-related stress. I believed he repressed things and perhaps with a little motivational tug here and there, I would be able to unlock the source of his problems and heal him. Initially, I was doing most of the talking. He didn't appear bothered by my sudden interest in talking more. But by the end of July, Curtis finally opened up. He told me something I never heard him say before.

"Something is missing. I can't put my finger on it, but I know it doesn't feel right. I'm miserable."

"What do you mean? You have a home, beautiful children, a good wife, and a well- paying job. What more could a man want? You have everything."

"I know, but I can't stop this feeling. It won't go away."

Like a good doctor, I prescribed things like relaxation and sleeping—things I thought would help improve our family situation and his mental state. As if the answer suddenly occurred to him, Curtis asked me to write the police a letter requesting the return of his guns.

"Sure, Curtis. If this will bring us peace, I 'll do it. What do you want me to write?"

He dictated verbatim as I wrote:

Dear Officer,

My name is Nusrat Brown and I am happily living with my husband and children since the incident on June 20, 1983. I no longer feel scared and I request that you return my husband's guns back to him. He served in Vietnam and risked his life serving his country. Thank you for your prompt decision.

Sincerely,
Nusrat Brown

One week later, a response from the court arrived for Curtis to appear in court. It wasn't connected to my letter, but the "gun to my heart" incident. Once more, his anger was ignited. I had heard stories of husbands with substance abuse problems that led them to commit heinous acts upon their wives. The morning before his court date was when the terror began all over again. My husband was sober which is why I never imagined his next move: shredding all my clothes.

When he came home from work around 4 a.m., I was already up. He walked into our bedroom, slammed the door, and started shredding everything I had with either his bare hands or his pocketknife.

"This is all your fault, Nusrat!"

He tore through my mink coat.

"See what you made me do?"

Then he reached for my cobra handbag.

"You're going to sit there and watch me do this."

He cut my underwear, my matching cobra slingback heels, even my books...all of my prized possessions except for the housedress on my back.

"You thought you could get my guns *taken* and that would be *it*?"

Sitting on the front edge of the bed for what felt like hours, I was too weak to beg him for mercy. With every rip, I felt as if I was physically injured. The emptiness in my soul created by the destruction made me feel like this was the end. At this moment, I was unable to mother or at least have the maternal instincts to worry about the kids in their bedroom just next door. Suddenly, I saw him stop in the middle of his rage to catch his breath.

His eyes zeroed in on the sight between my legs. He took a few steps before me and pinned me down on the bed. Unzipping his work pants, he spread my legs and mounted himself in me. The children were still sleeping until my shouting alarmed Yvonne.

"Mommy?"

I heard her voice at the bedroom door. I flinched, the blanket ruffled, and I tried to cover myself up quickly with the sheet. Fully aware of all my senses being bombarded, I drew a blank stare at the window and wasn't sure what to do next. Again I heard Yvonne call, "Mommy?"

This time, the sound of her voice was like a hypnotist's snap back into reality. Pushing Curtis' chest away, I maneuvered my hips as if to prevent his entry.

"Stop!" I begged him. "Yvonne's coming, she hears!"

He covered my mouth with his sweaty palm and said, "I could've bought more." With his other hand, he removed his pants and re-entered with a stronger force at a faster rate.

"Mommy?"

Her voice grew louder and I feared that at any moment she would knock on the door.

"Where are you?"

I heard the doorknob twisting and saw him searching for something on the side of the bed.

"Don't come in honey. Daddy wants you to obey."

I felt my breasts upon my chin as Curtis positioned my legs over his shoulders now.

"I could've just shot you, but then I thought stabbing you would hurt more."

Compressed together, I became numb to the rapid pounding.

"*Daddy* what are you doing?"

I heard Yvonne's voice through the door. Curtis stopped momentarily and continued grabbing my breasts as he slowed the momentum of his thrusts.

"I want you to suffer for how you made me suffer when the security guard looked at you," he said, placing the tip of the knife upon my heart, "and when you got my guns taken away."

I glanced at the knife before noticing his eyes were about to close. "Do *it!*"

He moved the metal tip away from my heart and to my bottom lip.

"You don't think I'll do it?" He pulled back and forced his pelvis harder into me. "I'll do it, Nusrat!"

He sounded like he was straining to take the top off a can, "Uh."

He kept the knife to my lip where it broke through the skin. Tasting blood as it dripped to the back of my throat, I feared I would choke. So I spit it out into his face.

"Do it, you fucking lunatic!"

Picking up my hand from the bed, he drew my index finger into his mouth and sucked.

"Should I cum Nusrat or should I stab you dead?"

I then felt the onslaught of him pounding into me faster and stronger until he finally climaxed. Closing my eyes, I fell into a pain-induced coma and then I heard Yvonne's voice filled with fear.

"Mommy? Daddy! Stop!!!"

The two-year-old slept through it all, but the cries from the crib indicated the baby's response to what was taking place. I immediately realized what Yvonne had witnessed: her father raping me while threatening to stab me.

"NO!" Yvonne screamed.

"NO!" I shrieked so loud that the neighbors phoned the police. Just as before, the cops whisked Curtis away in his briefs. An officer took us from our home, now a crime scene, and to Amy's house. Wearing their pajamas, the children and I waited for a ride to the Crisis Center on Amy's porch.

It was a Friday morning where the humidity hadn't set in yet. Within hours, the August heat would be unbearable. There we were, still on the porch, speechless. It wasn't like all the other times when we spoke about her husband's drinking and smoking or Curtis' shameful habit of reporting expired license plate tag numbers to the authorities. No, it was a time where things finally got out of control and could no longer be covered up. Waiting for a caseworker to transport us back to the Crisis Center felt like forever. I nursed Kevin while Darlene sat at my feet grabbing for the bottom of my housedress and Yvonne stood next to me. How pitiful did we look? The view of the back of my home showed all the windows in our apartment opened. No wonder Amy heard everything. I didn't see myself ever returning there again.

I didn't know what to say to Amy. The situation was so delicate. We just sat quietly. Then, she took the children inside her home and then returned back to me on the porch. "The children are having a little something."

"Thank you. I don't know what to say right now. I can't believe this is happening. I just want my family together. What's so wrong with that?"

"I know and I want you to know that I see Yvonne like the daughter I never had. Anytime you want to bring her here, I would be happy to spend time with her."

Yvonne popped up at the porch. Amy reached down and rubbed her head, "Right honey, you like spending time with Auntie Amy, don't you? You know you're like a daughter to me?"

Then she turned to me and said, "As long as I'm here, I will help you. This is what neighbors are for." She hugged me tighter, "You're not alone in this." Amy let go of my embrace and looked at me as if to make sure I was paying attention, "I feel like God put you here not just as my neighbor, but also as a sister."

My mind was overturned with what I prayed was the final blow from the physical, mental, and emotional abuse I had endured so long. I felt the tears coming. "I can't go through this anymore."

Amy took a deep breath and quickly exhaled. "I know I have to be strong for you and the children, Nusrat. I know it's not the time for me to get caught up in my emotions, but to see you with bruises on your face is unbearable."

I had no idea how many times Amy heard me screaming and begging Curtis to stop beating me up.

"I prayed one of your tenants would have gotten tired of hearing you fight and would call the police. But that never happened."

"They were afraid of being evicted."

"I've slept many nights feeling guilty. I listened to my husband's advice about not getting involved with your private affairs. But when I heard you screaming from my opened bedroom window, 'He has a knife! He has a knife!' I drew the line and called the police. I couldn't live with myself if something happened to you and the children. I know how Mr. Brown is," Amy paused and made direct eye contact with me, "I've heard you all the way from my living room and it just kills me. Please let me be there for you." Amy rubbed my shoulders, "Do you hear me Nusrat?"

I nodded, but that was all I could do as I stood frozen in disbelief. I was able to process everything I heard, but I was at a loss and embarrassed that Amy had known so much about my marriage. My throat tightened as I fought back my emotions, but I couldn't hold back the tears that wouldn't stop coming.

"Yvonne shouldn't see these things." Amy cried turning her face away from the child, "Nusrat, what are we going to do?"

"How am I going to do this by myself?" I flinched at the sound of the question. "Tonight, we will sleep again in the shelter. How am I going to care for my *three* children? How am I supposed to live like this?"

Ms. Rose, the same intake officer as before, checked us in again. How did I appear to her? Like a ruin, a spent force, a woman who was both alive and dead. Unlike our first meeting, I now sat wearing a ripped housedress instead of a polished suit. Taking a deep breath, I found it difficult to look her in the eye but began speaking anyway. "There is a hole in me. A big empty hole. I've worked hard at filling it with love, but for what? I'm here again. Just like you predicted."

I prayed Ms. Rose heard the defeat in my voice, the hopelessness that had finally overtaken me completely. Curtis had put a gun to my heart, a knife to my chest and lips, and forced himself on me too many times to count. Sitting in the chair across from Ms. Rose I said, "If a person can shred my clothes, then they can shred me."

This is where I would have cried, but I didn't even have the energy to do so.

"You were right. I get it now."

We sat for several minutes while I looked down and collected myself. Ending the silence, I said in a quiet voice filled with despair, "So now, how do I file a divorce? Tell me something about the process."

"Well, you can first begin by not looking at it like it's the end of the world. You can go to school, get a job, and raise your kids."

"But *I am* educated, I'm no stranger to the workforce. With all this, my children need a mother now more than ever. I have no problem being a housewife and taking care of my family."

"If you didn't have a problem managing your family Mrs. Brown, then quite frankly you wouldn't be here, would you? But I'm going to see to it that you get the help and resources that you need. This is going to include therapy."

I didn't know exactly what she meant by therapy. It's not like I was crazy. But I went along with whatever she said to get the help I knew the kids needed.

"An intern from our facility has picked up a bag filled with all of your ripped belongings to take them to your husband's court hearing. We are confident that Mr. Brown will not get his weapons back."

CHAPTER SIXTEEN

On September 25, 1983, Curtis showed up in court without an attorney. Therefore, the hearing was rescheduled for October 8, 1983, where the court awarded me the use and possession of the home. In other words, our official separation began. Curtis, who now stayed with his mother, started popping up unannounced to the house. At a whim, he would take the younger children from the front living room window to spend time with them. He knew my every move. I felt like he was spying on me especially when he knew I was cooking in the kitchen facing the back of the house. When I wasn't home, Amy told me of countless times she saw him driving by or walking around the house.

I made sure the shades were drawn at all times and that we walked by the entryway to not interrupt the light under the door. For God's sake, this man was preparing me for an early grave. Living in this type of fear was undoubtedly going to kill me if Curtis didn't do it first. I always felt his eyes on me. There were regular close calls in which the careless scrape of a chair against the hardwood floor or the dropping of a fork or something that would usually be overlooked would create a feeling of dread. Would he finally break into the apartment? It seemed that would be his next step. Gasping in fear over the fact that he was capable of anything, I felt like I was continuously losing my mind. This tension reminded me of the days leading up to our narrow escape from Iran, a time of tremendous suffering.

Keeping my animosity towards Curtis from the children was a challenge. I promised myself that I would mask as much of the pain as I could silently. Hence, I became an expert at hiding my fears: telling the children that the lights were low to save energy and that treading lightly in the house was the same as showing God that they were his humble servants. And although only Yvonne appeared terrified at the sporadic activities from her father, all of the children adapted to the new restrictions.

My days were filled with uncertainty and my nights were plagued by reoccurring dreams of snakes. Sometimes, I'd wake up to the sound of Curtis banging on the bedroom window for no reason but to scare me to death, to disrupt my life. I asked my attorney and caseworker, "What's the point of a restraining order if it doesn't protect me? He comes whenever he wants. How was I supposed to live like this?" But there wasn't much they could say to put me at ease except that I was following the appropriate steps to put an end to my marriage. All the while I desperately searched for what the laws really meant and how they were supposed to aid me and the children.

Ms. Rose, who was now like an extended family member, guided me through the separation process. Emphasizing the importance of employment, she encouraged me to take more computer training courses. She advised me to apply for minimum wage positions, like childcare and secretarial work, jobs I had no interest in working. Surely, I could find a computer job somewhere that would take my experience, but I was wrong. Most companies frowned upon my Iranian work history and required that I obtained U.S. training to be considered for employment. For God's sake, I was perfectly competent, so much that I could run all their businesses better. I had no idea why this was happening to me. Deep down I believed a job would hurt more than help.

If I got a 9-5, I would make money, but who would take care of my three children? Would I work just to pay for childcare? What sense did that make? Then my attorney reminded me that it would be in my best interest to secure a job. I needed to show the court that I was fit and able to provide a stable environment for the children. In my heart, I believed that I would be able to find work at the mosque. It was worth a try. So, I planned on visiting the Imam to see about a position. But just like most of my plans these days, this too would be delayed and threatened by Curtis' out of control behavior. I prayed for the day that he would let us move on. I needed to the space from him to figure out my new life. Thankfully I had Amy to look over the house to the extent that she could. Her comforting words "don't worry, everything will work out," made me feel better. I wish I knew when my luck was going to change.

However, my caseworker was persistent and her gentle threats loomed in my mind. Her questions were overwhelming: "Did you apply for WIC? For food stamps? How will you clothe the children? Do you have friends that can help?"

Of course, I applied for WIC and food stamps. I didn't have access to Curtis' bank accounts. The children still had to eat. Luckily, I was able to clothe us from the generous mosque donations and Amy. Ms. Rose's reminders for me to be "stable and financially secure" and prove I was a "competent mother" was all the pressure I needed to act fast.

As soon as I could, I made an appointment with the Imam. Thank God he was able to see me the next day. It had been years since I worked or discussed my qualifications. I wanted to make sure I said everything right. Though I was nervous, something inside of me felt like the mosque was where I should be. The next morning I dropped the children off and made my way to my meeting. When I got off the bus, I could only see one car in the parking lot. I guess this was to be expected since it was a Thursday. I was on time, 9 o'clock on the dot. The Imam welcomed me in from the entrance. Then, I followed him to his office.

"Thank you for taking the time to meet with me, Imam Ibrahimi," I said taking a seat.

"My pleasure, Sister, what can I do for you?"

"My husband and I are recently separated," I said as I wondered how I was going to describe the immediate nature of my situation.

Imagine my nerves, I had never spoken with him directly and didn't expect him to be familiar with me and the children. Then the voice of my caseworker popped into my mind: *Nusrat, you must show the court that you have the means and mental capacity to take care of your children. You have to get a job. Otherwise, you risk losing custody down the road.*

"My Crisis Center advocate said I have to work," I said as I lowered my eyes ashamed to face the Imam.

"I'm sorry, what do you mean?"

Then, as if in one giant gulp, the facts tumbled out quickly but with difficulty: "He tried to kill me. He cut my clothes. I have three children and we've been in and out of a women's shelter twice in the past six months. If I don't find a job, I could lose my children. With my oldest daughter starting first grade and the other two with a babysitter, I thought it would be a good idea to start seeking employment."

I couldn't believe what I heard coming from my lips: my reality, a life filled with endless tragedy. I stopped before I said another word.

Wedging its way into a standstill, the all too familiar brief moment of silence came upon us. Did he want to know about my family back home? Was the Imam uncomfortable? Was he going to ask me more about my husband?

Then he said, "I am sorry this is happening."

"Me too, I married my husband back home. Then, we came here because of the Revolution. I love my children, but I had no idea that my life would turn out like this. I didn't make them by myself." Covering my eyes with both hands, I took a deep breath to control the tears pulsing in my throat. "And now everything is on me. Please tell me that you have a position open."

"The mosque's budget is tight since we are working on collecting money for the expansion. I do not want to feel responsible, though, if something were to happen to you and your three children. I'm sure we can arrange something for you, Sister. Do you do secretarial work?"

"Yes," My eyes perked up. "I also speak Farsi, my mother tongue, and read and write Arabic. Based on my experience, I can teach Farsi, history, geography, and religious classes. I am also able to perform duties in any administrative capacity." I made eye contact with the Imam to see if he was impressed. "I have experience with computers as well." I paused to think of what else I could share. "I can also help in the daycare center, anything you need."

"Let me talk to some of the Brothers and Sisters and see what we can do for you. Until then, remember Allah and always give thanks."

That January, I secured a secretarial position for $2.50 per hour at the mosque. It was a hopeful way to begin the new year. The hourly rate wasn't anything close to what I had earned in Iran, but I thanked Allah for it. Things were finally falling in place naturally for our greater good. While I worked, the younger two were in daycare and Yvonne was in school. If and when I got into a childcare bind, Amy would help out. Oddly, I felt as if I was set up for success. The first two weeks on the job were nearly perfect. There was nothing for me to do except file receipts, order Sunday school supplies, and answer the phone which now made me uneasy.

Two days prior, on Friday right before prayer, a woman called in a panic about her sister who had been murdered by her husband. Distraught and entirely at a loss as to how to handle this tragedy, the woman knew to call the only mosque in the metropolitan area, The Islamic Community Center. She frantically asked me, "Is there a place Muslims can be buried? Who will wash the body? Can this be done in 24 hours? Who can perform the last rites? How much will these things cost?"

Every question stirred an element of anxiety which ignited a firework of emotions. It was similar to what I felt leaving the Crisis Center and going to the Imam for help. Now faced with the distraught sister of the murdered woman, I searched the mosque resources to try and aid her. It wasn't like there was a list relating to rites readily available. No *death manual* so to speak. It had been so long since I worked under pressure like this, but I fell into it with such a passion that one would think I had been working at the mosque for a lifetime. I ran through the membership Rolodex and made cold calls until I had gained enough information to help the woman. Immersing myself in the situation so thoroughly, I almost missed the bus to pick Yvonne up from school. Luckily, the Imam gave me a ride.

For the first time since I came to America, I had a genuine feeling of being valued. After speaking with Sister Mariam, I received interview questions necessary to create the death announcement from Imam Ibrahimi. I called her again.

"Please Mariam, kindly give me your sister's name. I'm afraid I need some information to put the death announcement together."

"Sh—Shireen…Shireen Khan," she replied, stammering as if on the verge of breaking.

I continued, "Age?"

"Thirty."

"Education?"

"High school. We, I mean, she went to a school back home in Afghanistan."

At this point, I fell silent. I was just three years older than Shireen, Miriam's dead sister. I remembered the posters at the Crisis Center of missing people and how the news reported that Shireen had been a victim of an abusive relationship. I left the scripted questions and asked how she died. Mariam told the story of how the family had fallen on hard times and how being an immigrant with limited resources only got worse when the three children came. She spoke of how sad it was to see the decent man that Shireen's husband once was had begun to shut himself off from the world after losing his job. Miriam feared the worst when her sister had not called her in the last week of December. Now, here she was calling the mosque for funeral arrangements. The doctors had told her the day before that the internal bleeding was untreatable and Shireen's condition was grave. They had even said she wouldn't make it to the weekend.

The thought of meeting such a fate crossed my mind not long before. I filed it away in my heart until now. Perhaps God was keeping me alive for the sake of my children? I believed in seven years of bad luck when a mirror cracked, in the cleansing power of burning frankincense, and in dropping off bags of clothes at the steps of the Baptist church down the street from my home. Of course, these were my private beliefs that I kept to myself and shielded them from the Imam. For this reason, I took the phone call experience as a sign for me to get my affairs in order. Immediately, I made an appointment with a man from a nearby funeral home to visit and make my own arrangements. Exhausted from taking care of the children by myself, I had to face that I was in fact *still* alive. And yet I never thought of death as a possibility until Miriam's phone call. While I had feared for my life many times before, the idea of Curtis killing me became real. And to think this woman didn't know where to turn. Helping her only made my fears run wild with unimaginable thoughts. Who would handle my affairs if I died of natural causes or worse if Curtis shot me dead? Was he capable of retaliating in this way now that he was forced to pay for everything? He wouldn't leave us alone. What if he was just waiting for the right time?

By now I had worked for five months and was separated for seven months. It was the first Saturday in May 1984 and I was prepared to have a quiet night at home when a thunderstorm shook Takoma Park. Flashes of lightning hit the grass from the dark sky above. The thunder was so loud it sounded like it was coming from within the house. After putting the children to bed in my room, I sat in the living room. Curtis came to mind when I sat in his favorite spot for watching television with a gallon of rum raisin ice cream on his lap. Looking out the window, I found the thunder to be unusually soothing. What would I do now? Would I ever have peace? I searched the front yard as if it would give me the answers. Opening the window, I welcomed the hissing winds and the spray from the blinding torrential rain.

Then a figure came from the hallway headed towards me, it was Yvonne, who burst into tears and fell into my lap. "Mommy, I'm scared."

She faced the window and said "What's happening? Is daddy here?"

"Shhh honey, it's okay and no, he's not here, it's just a storm."

"But my friend told me about storms and lightning and I don't want to die."

"Die? You're not going to die." I said holding her tight and kissing her forehead until she returned to sleep. I remembered her as a baby and how despite being so alone and far away from family, the love and anticipation of having my first child had carried and sustained me through a difficult pregnancy. And how I loved my baby so much, that sacrificing my own life in exchange for my daughter to grow up in America was hard, but worth it. I remembered how the bundle of joy nestled only on my chest and cried when anyone else had reached to hold her. It was a true badge of motherhood that my presence was all my little one needed to experience comfort. Now, I carried Yvonne to my room, where I shared a king size bed with three children.

Tonight, Curtis didn't bang at my bedroom window. But, just as I prepared for bed, the nearby sound of fire engines and ambulances distracted me from entering deep sleep. In the middle of the night, Kevin, the youngest, woke up vomiting. I washed him up then propped his head against slanted pillows. I watched his little face until I finally dozed off into a sleep deep enough to dream of snakes again.

Never did they attack; I usually woke up right before they struck. This one was an aggressive anaconda with red glowing eyes. Frightened and out of breath at nearly being killed, I sat up in the bed trying to figure out what was happening. Why were they haunting my subconscious? Remembering what my grandfather told me to do if I ever had a bad dream, I spit once to the left and once to the right while reciting the prayer, Surah Fatihah.

The night before, I dreamed of an albino python in a coiled position unmoving in his white and yellow skin. The fire from his red eyes struck me as he slowly leaned forward and I finally awoke. Growing up, my aunties told me of a time I was almost attacked by a snake while on holiday in Bombay. Sitting in front of a fireplace, a servant had held me in her arms in the bungalow. A snake dangled down from the fireplace with his head exposed and lunged for my face, unknown to the servant. It was then that my mother rushed toward the servant and snatched me from her arms; the startled snake darted back up the chimney. Aside from this family tale, snakes were not a part of my waking life. And yet anytime I woke up from a dream to catch my breath, I had a desperate sense of what snakes symbolized. Death.

I awoke the following morning feeling as though the weight of my heavy heart made it impossible to get out of my bed. I reached for my notepad off the nightstand and jotted down my dreams and snake descriptions. I hoped to spot a pattern and make sense of why the serpents plagued my mind.

Putting my notepad away, I got up to face the morning. I fixed Cream of Wheat for breakfast while the children watched Saturday morning cartoons. Lowering the burner, I added butter to the pot and went to call them to the table. Next, I heard a loud bang from what I thought was from the front door. With all of Curtis' unlawful entries and continued threats, my life in the house was unbearable. I walked towards the living room to see about the door. I held the potential for misfortune in my tight chest. Entering the living room, I caught Yvonne leaning out the window with the screen up. She said to her father, "You're a bad daddy."

Then she raised her hand and slapped her father right in the face. I stared at my child. I couldn't think of what would make my sweet-natured daughter do such a thing. And my hatred for him intensified for bringing this out of her, an innocent child.

"What's going on here?" I pulled Yvonne back in the house." What are you doing here?" I snapped the screen window closed. With the window being five feet above ground, Curtis didn't pose an immediate threat. "You're not supposed to be here! It's in the court order! Today is *not* your day for visitation and *nothing* needs to be fixed, so *leave!*"

I grabbed Yvonne and was about to warn him that I was going to call the police. And then I stopped myself, turned sharply, and headed for the kitchen. The two younger kids sat crying on the couch. Curtis leaped toward the window and punched a hole through the screen with his bare hands. I reported to the operator, "My husband is here trying to kill me!" Before I hung up the phone, Curtis had pulled himself up into the house through the window. Just as my eyes met him, I gasped, "Please don't hurt us."

I put Yvonne behind me, using my body as a shield. He calmly approached us.

"Yvonne, daddy just wants to visit you, darling. Don't you miss daddy? That wasn't nice what you did to daddy's face."

I leaned back closer against her, "She's just a child. She doesn't know what she's doing Curtis."

"You're right, Nusrat. I want all of you to know I love you and that I don't like this situation. It's not good for anyone."

He relaxed his face putting me slightly at ease.

"Let's see how I can fix the window," he said.

Just as he walked down the hallway, I ran to my bedroom. From my window, I saw the police pull up to the house. I was sure Curtis had seen them by now while he was "fixing" the ripped screen. The Cream of Wheat was now burning. As I went to remove the pot from the heat, I overheard him speaking to the officers. He assured them that he was only in the house to repair the window and that he was permitted to do so under the recent court order.

"I'm almost done here and then I'll leave." I heard Curtis say to the children.

That son of a bitch thinks he can do whatever he wants. I walked back in the room surprised to see the officers helping him manage the window. "Officer, why is he still here? He is going against a court order *and* a restraining order."

"Ma'am, he's almost done fixing the window. We will be out of your way shortly."

Curtis pulled the whole screen out and said, "I'll have to get another one from Hechinger's. I hope they still carry this size."

And with a wink of an eye, he walked out the front door. Neglecting to say bye to the children, he waved to the police, who were already waiting in their cars until he left the property.

Unsure if I should tell the police that I placed the call, I walked out the house. Yes, they would want to know how Curtis was the one who vandalized the window, and how he had used making repairs an excuse to continue terrorizing me and the children. I felt they needed to understand better how I feared for my life and the children's safety. Maybe they would hear my desperate plea and imagine their sister or mother in a similar position. Perhaps they'd do everything in their power to see the court order would be followed.

Instead, the police officer got in his car and pulled off driving down Garland Avenue. All I could do was stand on the front lawn and cry. A small piece of me wanted to believe the police car followed him to make sure he wouldn't return or to lock him up for breaking the court order. But they didn't return until the next time I called for breaking and "fixing" yet another window, then the front and kitchen doors, and the broken furniture which now cluttered the living room. Why didn't they believe me when I said he was the one doing all of this?

I was changing locks to the house every month with money I didn't have. How long was it going to take for the cops, lawyers, and the court to notice Curtis' repairs were exclusive to my apartment and never to the other two tenants? When would it finally occur to them how odd it was that my two-bedroom apartment required so much repair of broken furniture, doors, and windows? At first, an outsider may have found Curtis' behavior laughable, almost child-like. He didn't cut the gas line or start fires *yet*. It was just a matter of time before he did something crazy. It was menacing and the end to his shit was nowhere in sight.

⇥⇤ ⇥⇤

It was a warm Thursday morning in July when a lady came to the mosque office asking me to teach her three children the Quran. She said they were too young for Sunday school and wanted me to do it at her house. I heard her, but I really didn't pay attention to what she was asking.

"Sister Nusrat, do you remember me? I am Mariam; you helped me when my sister died."

My chest tightened. "Yes, of course, I remember you. How are you? How is your family?"

"We are managing Mashallah. Her death put life into perspective. I want my children to know the Quran."

I was balancing my job, going to court, dodging eviction, and dealing with the children when her request came in and out of my ears. I gave her a list of Brothers that were teaching the Quran. I wish I could have helped her more, but I was already spreading myself thin. After seeing the Sister out, I continued my work when the words *freedom is a rose petal many died for* popped into my mind. What did it mean?

Later that afternoon, the man from the funeral home visited. I had made three previous appointments to see him, but all had to be rescheduled. Something was always coming up between Curtis and the kids. The two younger children were visiting with their father and Yvonne had just finished cleaning the apartment when I answered a knock at the door.

Dressed in a black suit with freshly polished black shoes and a black briefcase, the funeral man's smile was as wide as the shine on his bald head. He looked like a thin version of Uncle Fester from the Adams Family show. I invited him into the living room and offered him a cup of tea. He acknowledged Yvonne with an awkward smile as if her presence made him uncomfortable. When I returned with a drink, he already had his briefcase opened with various flyers and documents prepared for signatures set on the coffee table. Yvonne sat quietly as we got down to business deciding on plot location and finally payment arrangements. Conducting this business in front of her, I believed was necessary, a real-life experience to help her grow. I hoped she would mature quicker or re-member this time when she got older to appreciate her mother's struggle and sacrifice. Perhaps she would one day grieve for Iran and her parents' failed marriage. Maybe she could feel my pain as a shunned foreigner without a clue as to how to raise three American children. Yvonne should know I was taking care of this now, so she wouldn't have to do it later.

"Can you handle $11 a month?" He asked in his closing sales pitch. "This is the best offer we have. You could have it paid off in four years and be at peace knowing this is taken care of."

My God, it would take me four hours of work just to afford the $11 payment. I barely made enough for basic necessities like toilet paper and shampoo. Then I thought about what it would look like making extra money teaching the Quran. I laughed at myself and forgot about it. No matter the setback, this was important and I had to make it work.

My mind drifted and then I heard Yvonne sniffling. The straps to her overalls were sliding over her shoulder. I got up from my seat plac-ing them correctly and hugged her, "It's okay Sweetie, don't cry." I waited for her to calm down. "Yvonne, your father is gone, we're all we have. I know this may be hard for you, but what can I say? This is our life. You're the oldest. God has blessed you with being mature beyond your years. If something happens to me, you're in charge."

The man from the funeral home interrupted and asked me what was to be inscribed on my tombstone. I replied, "Yvonne, what do you think should be on it?"

Yvonne looked at me in disbelief.

"Mom, what do you want me to do?"

"I know it isn't easy, but it's important."

At a loss for words, my poor daughter ran to her room and cried herself to sleep. When she woke up, the man was long gone and I was cooking dinner. She entered the kitchen looking for me to stop what I was doing.

"Mommy, I don't know how to say this, but it feels like I'm hurting inside."

"I'm sorry honey," I bent down and gave her a hug and kiss, "but your mother has diabetes now. And I have so much to take care of. You understand, don't you?"

"Does that mean you're dying?"

"No, of course not. But I have to take care of things. We are alone in this country."

I repeated it over and over again that I wasn't dying. And though it looked like my words brought Yvonne relief, she would remind me about "the pain in her little heart."

I felt like I merely existed as if a light had died inside of my soul. Until one day Yvonne transformed right before my eyes. It was as if our roles changed and she was now the mother. She said to me, "I'm going to help you live. I'm going to take care of you. Don't worry. We at least have each other."

I really don't know what I would have done without my daughter, so full of love and hope. She helped me with her siblings and with the house, and now she took on the role as my light. Selling brownies to the neighbors, she became quite the entrepreneur. Yvonne was never the cause of my stress. I was a lucky mother.

After six months, the Sister from the mosque asked me again about teaching her children. She looked thirty, close to my age, but I got the feeling that she knew me more than what she wanted me to think. It felt like our ties went beyond the experience of her sister's death. I asked her where she lived and learned she wasn't far from my home. I didn't know where she got the idea that I could teach her children. Then it all made sense when she told me how she and her mother used to pray in my grandmother's home in Iran. It was all so strange. How did she associate me with being the granddaughter of Bibi Joon?

"I know you are qualified to teach my children the Quran Sister Nusrat." She insisted.

The last thing I needed was to be the first woman in this area to teach the Quran. I was already in the public eye because my life was in court. Just covering my head drew unwanted attention. I didn't need a platform or the pressure. I wasn't a public person and I had no interest in putting myself out there. I responded to her request by saying, "I've never taught the Quran before. Maybe you should find another teacher."

"Thank you Sister, but I believe you are the best teacher."

I didn't have experience teaching the Quran, but my grandfather did teach me how to read and recite when I was five. I remembered him opening the book in front of me asking me to "read" and nothing had come out of my mouth. From that point, he taught me twice a week. I grew comfortable asking him for help. He read and then I read it after him, this was how I learned to recite the Quran. There wasn't much to it. Maybe I could teach a child in the same way?

I asked the Sister to bring me an Arabic book to study. Once I began going through it, I was amazed at how much knowledge came to me on how to teach it to another person. For the first time, I seriously considered this as a potential job. But with all that I had going on, I had to decline again.

Curtis and I were separated from 1983-1985 before our divorce was finalized on April 24, 1986. During this time, I pursued at least two criminal complaints against him for breaking the protective order. Also, I sought police intervention on countless occasions for verbal assault and battery. Toward the end of the divorce battle, it came out that I had purchased a burial plot. The judge asked me why I had bought it. I reminded the court that fearing my husband would kill me was a reality I lived with every day. I purchased my plot to secure some sort of dignity in death. But Curtis insisted that I was always planning to take the children to Iran and never return. I thought he said this to the court to gain favor regarding custody. Regardless, I remained firm in my position; America was the land of my children and the place where *I* would be buried.

A camel collapses. Waiting for water...

CHAPTER SEVENTEEN

I felt the ruffled hem of my pink and purple floral house dress over my knees. After putting my hair in a ponytail, I paced the living room in search of a fan. It was the spring of 1987 and President Reagan accepted full responsibility for how the Iran Arms-Contra policy went wrong. Ever since the divorce last year, Curtis stopped providing. Whatever the Department of Social Services was able to help with was quite minimal compared to the level of our need. I caught a glimpse of my fan between the children's toys on the floor. Opening it up, I was surprised the children hadn't destroyed it and that it was still useable. At least I had this to bring me some relief from the heat.

It was all about survival now. It was all about making it from one day to the next. How could he just cut me off? I was the mother of his children. Did that mean anything? Was this par for the course? Was there any justice on this earth? Still, I was suffocating in my misery. The only sound was the flapping, repetitive sweep of my fan, like the wings of a seagull approaching land and unlike me, free. All around me, the furniture my parents purchased marked with memories of how we failed at making a life together.

The rising sun began to glow around the heavily draped window. In the break of the morning, dressed in flowers, I felt fresh and imagined I looked like a walking botanical garden. A stark contrast to what life looked like now, one dramatic court order after another. I thought this would be behind me with the divorce, but I saw my madness was only beginning. I was raising children alone (something I didn't know was possible). With nothing to comfort me but the belief that God had given them to me and only He could take them away, I fought back desperate thoughts.

Yesterday, my lawyer called to share Curtis' response to me filing for child support. "He says you have demonstrated yourself an unfit person to care and have custody of the kids. He wants to sell the house because he claims he can't afford to maintain it and wants to decrease his expenses."

What kind of man would take the house from his children? It was too much for me to comprehend. I was a single-mother and divorcée. It seemed every promise made to me had been dishonored.

Yvonne, now 10, was by my side every step of the way. Just like she had done since she was little. She eased my burden. It was clear in the ways she availed herself. She learned how to properly sweep the kitchen floor, separate the colors from the whites, pack food in the refrigerator, and wash dishes. I taught her how to fix potato salad and pick her siblings up from school. All the while, if I wasn't in the bathroom crying, I was at the kitchen sink breaking down. Sometimes the kids noticed, but I grew to no longer care. My pain had to come out some way.

I turned, scratching my forehead and glanced at the family portrait framed in matching dark wood above the fireplace mantel. "Yvonne?" I called out. "Darlene? Kevin?"

I heard Yvonne's voice across the hallway. I waited, expecting all three of them would parade down the hallway at any minute. This wasn't a morning for fighting, bickering, or playing games. I wasn't going to spend all morning watching the congressional hearings. I called them again. My mind was overwhelmed with all I had to accomplish with the house chores, cooking, tenants, running errands, phone calls to the law-yer, and meeting with Crisis Center staff. Accomplishing all this while dragging the children from one place to another was beyond difficult. I surprised myself sometimes at what I was able to do.

The only relief I found was when Yvonne visited with her friends or when all three children were in school. After the divorce, I wasn't able to afford childcare, so I quit my job. Besides this, I was concerned about the younger ones who quickly established themselves in the eyes of the mosque, counselors, and school as unruly, out of control, even emotion-ally disturbed. Nevertheless, I was their mother and I did my best to work with them.

Unlike Yvonne, the other two needed me differently. It wasn't their fault that their father raped me when they were conceived. It wasn't their fault that he beat me while they were in my womb. It wasn't their fault that they weren't wanted and yet it pained me to look at them at times. These feelings were always intensified by the guilt I felt for having them. At times I felt like I wasn't capable of giving them what they needed and wished life for all of us could've been entirely different. But here we were.

I pulled the blind up and saw the next-door neighbor walking her dog in front of the house on the sidewalk. Our eyes met and then the lady pulled at her dog to walk faster. Soon they disappeared from my sight. Then Yvonne, with her amber-brown eyes, appeared in the living room. She was a replica of me and my mother. With her olive skin, thick curly black hair, and mature nature, she made me proud. Last week, she had caught lice from school and had to get her hair cut. She was hurt when kids at school teased her about looking like a boy. But, I reminded my child, "You're too pretty for someone to mistake you for a boy. Don't worry, it will grow back fast." I wasn't sure if my words registered in her mind, but I hoped they did.

The younger two children popped up behind Yvonne. I believed that with every day Darlene and Kevin grew to look more and more like their father. This was a fact I would remind them of whenever they wouldn't listen, used profanity towards adults, or broke something like the neighbor's window. I felt a pang of sorrow sometimes when I looked at them. Their faces were reminders of unspeakable regret that I had for returning to America with Curtis. In Yvonne, I still had hope that at least she could have a chance for something better, but at what cost? Everything was messed up. We were living in hell.

I sat down in awe of my children, not in the way a mother would necessarily be content, but in a way that brought a deep chord of torment. My children transformed into beings out of my control right before my eyes. Where Yvonne was once fearful of me, she now had a temper; where Darlene, age 6, once looked up to her sister, she now was a terror, even the three year old, who had slept and ate well, was now waking up several times in the middle of the night from nightmares. They all fought for my attention. I was just one person. What was I supposed to do? I couldn't cut myself in half. There was hardly anything left of myself to give. Why couldn't my children understand this fact?

In my life, so much was shattered now. With the children and all the uncertainty, I rarely had time to reflect or write anymore. "Come here," I said as I motioned them towards me sitting in the recliner. "I want you to wash up and get dressed. I'm taking you out the house. Maybe we can go to the park. If you hurry up and be good, I'll take you to McDonald's for ice cream."

Their eyes lit up and they ran to the bathroom where Yvonne washed them up and got them dressed. Waiting for the pot of coffee to brew, I sat by the window in the living room. I thought about how there weren't playgrounds in Iran when I was growing up. We only had the backyard garden. So relieved was I to have a car now, I promised myself that I would take the children to the Potomac Overlook Park, a place I saw once on my way to a member of the mosque's home. Exposing my children to beautiful places (far from their father) was the least I could do for them.

The park was in a neighborhood centered among mansions and filled with private school kids and their nannies. It was a long distance from our neighborhood in Takoma Park with its rising crime rate and drug problems. I calculated whether I had enough gas in the car to drive a half an hour to Potomac. Staring out the window, I remembered how Allah had blessed me with a car because of Yvonne. Yes, it was true, I had a way to get around, but every penny had to be counted.

Though it had been a year since I stopped working at the mosque, I still worshipped and attended social programs. I took the children to a mosque fundraising picnic. Curtis had kept the family car when he moved to his mother's home, leaving me with taking the bus as the only means of transportation. Of course, this limited my freedom and added the pressure of carrying the children around town through all types of weather. When we got to the mosque, I sat at a table to collect myself. My increasing weight made it more difficult for me to manage the children, so I let them run around and play while I kept a close eye on them. As the two little ones were playing, I spotted Yvonne waiting in line to get food. She was talking with Dr. Azal and Dr. Qalif, fathers of her Sunday school friends. I wondered what on earth she could be discussing with them as they appeared quite engaged with whatever she was saying. After what seemed like half an hour, they eventually walked over to me. Dr. Azal spoke first, "Hello Sister, you have quite a daughter. I must say I'm impressed with how mature she is, far beyond her years."

"Thank you, Brother Azal, yes, I'm proud of her."

"Yes, well, I was just discussing with Dr. Qalif about how I am getting a new car and that I was thinking about what to do with the one I currently have. This was when your daughter tapped me on the shoulder and told me that you did not have a car and that you only take the bus with your three small ones."

His words were like a match striking my face. I looked at Yvonne and saw her standing before me smiling as if expecting a pat on the head or a kiss on the cheek. I wanted nothing more than to slap her face for embarrassing me like this in front of the doctor.

"Sister, please understand your daughter is your best friend. She has so much compassion for you, which is why instead of selling my car, I want to give it to you."

"*Give?*"

"Yes, you heard me correct." He noticed my disbelief. "All you have to do is pay for the title and of course your car insurance and it is yours."

God is Provider. I wasn't going to ruin the moment by fretting about how I was going to pay for these things. Farewell to our bus riding days. Soon we would be in our very own white two-door Toyota Celica. When Dr. Azal gave me the keys, I cried.

"It is my pleasure Sister. I simply could not deny Yvonne."

It's true, Yvonne was my lucky charm. But more than that, she was my "good" child, proof that in the midst of the darkness, there was hope. I had to provide all of my children with the best I could. For now, that meant taking them to a park far away from home. Finally, they were dressed and ready to go.

"Thank you, Mommy, for taking us out," Yvonne said. "We're all ready."

Whenever I looked deep in thought or appeared sad, Yvonne would show her love by expressing appreciation. My face softened. "You are thanking me because I'm taking you out the house?" I got up to get my pocketbook from the coffee table. It was then that I noticed what the children were wearing: Darlene had on a short jean skirt, a long-sleeved polka dot shirt, and a pair of purple snow boots; Kevin wore a t-shirt with sweatpants and sandals, and Yvonne had on a green floor-length paisley skirt, a canary yellow wool vest that she wore as a shirt, and a pair of black shoes with a bit of a heel. Overtaken by the spectacle of my children, I wanted an answer from God as to why our life was this low. Exhaling one long frustrated breath from my weary chest, I pulled Darlene's skirt down. Next, I told Yvonne to get a pair of socks for Kevin to wear with his sandals. When Yvonne returned from the bedroom, I asked her if the shirt itched. She denied it and proceeded to scratch where the tag hit her neck.

"It's from Neiman Marcus Mommy and I like it."

"Come here." I rolled Yvonne's skirt up at the waist so it wouldn't hit the floor. "Where did you find these clothes?

"In the trash bag from the mosque. I think the rich doctors' wives donated a lot of their things."

"I see."

Then the heavy weight of despair came over me and I shook it off. I remembered when Yvonne was four, I had "Mommy and me" outfits made for her, along with other beautiful dresses. Though I never saw the sense in purchasing high-end clothes for children, I made it my business to always have enough to afford something brand-new, never used, from Sears. My children were growing at an alarming rate and on top of that, the younger ones tore up what little we had left. It was like their regular play always turned into something being messed up. A window, a door, a glass cup, anything in their path, would be broken, just like how their father damaged things.

"Okay, let's go. Let's get out of here." I wanted them to get out before I changed my mind. "Yvonne, take your brother and sister to the car, I'll be right behind you. I'm getting your snacks together. I'll be right there."

After a few minutes, I locked the door and prayed for the safety of our home. It was always on my mind that Curtis would come and do something. I set off down the walkway. Then I paused and guided myself toward the sound of my children yelling and fighting over the front seat.

"I'm the oldest," Yvonne warned her brother and sister.

I saw Yvonne kick her foot inside the car pushing Darlene out the way.

"That's why I must sit in the front. *Move!*"

Yvonne shoved Darlene into the back and took her seat in the front of the car. *Allah, You gave them to me and You must take them away!* The sound of the children bickering got louder as I approached the car door. I didn't know how to control them anymore. I cried without tears. *My children drove me crazy.*

"Get off me!" Darlene screamed.

"I'm not touching you," Yvonne said.

"I *said* get off!" She pushed Yvonne.

I got into the car and demanded Yvonne to stop fighting.

"If you don't leave me alone," growled Yvonne, "I'm going to hurt you."

"Yvonne, did you hear me?" I put the key in the ignition. "I want to take you guys to the park. Or do you want to stay home all day?"

They completely ignored me. I began to drive hoping the girls would stop fighting, but then it got worse. Darlene pushed a clump of mucus out her nose and smeared it on Yvonne's ear.

"That's what you get," Darlene said to her sister.

How could my child be so young and be so mean? "I need you guys to stop the fighting! Do you want me to get into an accident?"

In the corner of my eye, I caught Yvonne grabbing the car jack from the floor by her feet. "What are you doing Yvonne?"

From the front seat, Yvonne rammed the pointy metal corner of the jack into Darlene's knee. Her punctured knee, I'm sure was bleeding. Yvonne turned her head back to the front to see if I realized what she had done. Turning to the back seat again, she promised Darlene, "When you're eighty years old and your legs are propped up, you will remember this moment, *Prick Face.*"

My children were officially unruly. Thoughts of our future zoomed in my mind. How would I provide a life for them? How would they would eat? How would I wash their clothes?

"Do you want me to take you to the police station? Do you want to go to jail? Do you want your father to take care of you? Do you want me to leave you here and go back to Iran by myself?"

"No mommy no! We'll be good." They all insisted. This would be all they needed to be scared, but it never lasted long.

"That's it!" I finally said, "I'm taking you to the police station." And when we arrived in the parking lot, the two younger ones generally straightened up until we headed back home, then it would start all over again.

As each day passed, I believed my children were growing needier and worse behaved. How could I begin to help them? I hoped to teach them compassion for others by making sandwiches for the homeless. I would drive through DC searching for people to feed and have the children help pass food out. I tried my best to be a good mother although it felt I had failed. How could I teach them with all the worries on my mind? How could I make a life with all I was now responsible for? And what about Yvonne? The boys were already giving her stares. Another job on my already crowded list of things to manage.

With this, I thought it was an appropriate time to teach my daughter the importance of marriage. I was going to scare her straight and let her know any relationship with a man outside of marriage would send her straight to hell. Of course, I wanted her to be educated, but there was more stability in the home. I made it a point to let her know if she fancied something, my response would always be, "I'll buy that for you when you get married."

Pleading with God to guide my soul, I prayed Yvonne would never become like the loose teenagers I had seen on the television. I knew she wasn't interested in boys yet, but her body was maturing at a faster speed than her mind.

A week after the children's car fight, I was watching the 5 o'clock news. Yvonne stood in front of me holding out an 8X10 photo obstructing my view. I could've slapped her to the ground. "Mom," she said. "You look so pretty."

I took the picture and looked at it, and there we were, her father and me while I was pregnant on her in Iran. My aggravation softened and I felt sorry for my child. Yvonne, however sweet, had eyes that seemed to be losing their twinkle. "That's me and your father in Iran when I was pregnant with you." I said as if recalling the memory didn't make me upset. Admittedly, she had seen enough by now to know better and not be fooled.

"You mean I'm in there?" She pointed to my belly in the picture.

I nodded, "Yes, that's you."

The picture began to make me angry, so I reached to get it from her and put it away, but she grew more excited. "You and daddy are smiling."

She said. "Was it because *I* was in *your* tummy?" She looked up at me for a response.

"Of course it is." I pulled Yvonne into a hug and watched her beam at the realization that once upon a time, her parents smiled at the thought of her existence.

"Mommy." She held my cheeks close, "I only want to see you smile."

Experiencing anything close to happiness wasn't possible. Nothing made me smile anymore, not even my children. I did my best to carry on as usual for them, but it was true that our everyday existence was unbearable. I had given in to my horrible life. Now, it was evident by the permanent scowl on my face. In some pictures, I had seen this face even when I was trying to smile.

⟫⟨ ⟩⟫

Just like all the other summer nights, the children and I passed the time in the evening watching the television until something happened to Yvonne. I asked her to get me a glass of water. When she returned with it, I asked her to go back to the kitchen, "You know I like my water cold. What's wrong with you?"

She returned, finally with the ice water.

"Here mommy. I'll be back, I have to go to the bathroom."

I watched Yvonne walk to the bathroom and noticed with almost a new set of eyes how my daughter was growing up both physically and mentally. For her to only be ten years old, she had a full budding breast, a shape in her hips, and plumpness in her behind that reminded me of when I became a young woman. She looked like she left childhood behind almost overnight. When I was her age, I grew a full size overnight and never returned to being small again. I didn't want her to have the same weight problem I had at an early age. But her curves were already pronounced with the anticipation of her body maturing into full-blown womanhood.

Yes, she ran the house, but she was still *my* child. It was my duty to save her from teenage pregnancy and find her a husband. I got up to change the channel for the kids when I heard her screaming from the bathroom.

"What's wrong Yvonne?"

"Mommy! Please come! Now!"

"I'm coming, are you okay?" I went to open the door, but it was locked. "Yvonne, I'm here, open the door."

"Hold on." She opened the door and returned to sitting on the toilet.

"What's the matter with you?"

"I went to the bathroom and when I pulled my panties down, I saw this."

It was brownish blood. *Oh my God*, I wanted to remain calm, but I couldn't help but panic. I was sure this made the situation worse.

"Mommy, I'm bleeding! I mean, I'm having a baby! Just like those girls on Donahue. I'm dying! Help me!"

"Yvonne, you're *not* dying and you're *not* having a baby."

"Then what's happening? Why am I bleeding?"

"It's normal. It's what happens to girls when they become women."

My fear of her becoming pregnant had intensified. I went into her room to get a clean pair of underwear and returned to the bathroom. Yvonne sat, still in tears. "Don't cry, Honey. Take a shower and put these on. Everything is going to be okay."

With all of our interaction in the court now, Curtis and I no longer spoke on the phone. Despite this fact, I went into the kitchen to call her father anyway. This act, no matter how difficult, was mandatory. There was no lawyer in the world qualified to deal with our daughter getting her period.

"You have to come here and get your daughter," were the first words that came out of my mouth. "I don't know what to do. In my country, we get them married at once. She has her period now. I don't want her to be one of these girls that gets pregnant because her father isn't around."

"What are you talking about? Do you hear yourself? Can you just relax and think logically (for once)? That didn't happen to you. You didn't get married once you got yours."

"Good, I'm glad you have all the answers. And no, I don't want to relax. Come fix this."

"What am I supposed to do Nusrat?"

"I can't do this by myself anymore. I have to figure out how I'm going to pay for food, apply for food stamps, when to wash them, comb their hair, help them with their homework, sign permission slips, go to my job, repair the house, deal with your shit and now this child has her period? And you can just live your life. Dash off into the sunset like nothing ever happened? Like I did this all by myself? No. *You* come and *fix* this. Now!"

"You don't want me around the house. If I come to see my kids, you call the police. You're not letting me help you. If you lightened up a little, all of this wouldn't be so bad."

"She's your daughter too. I didn't make her by myself. I don't even have the money for maxi-pads for myself. What makes you think I don't need help?"

"Alright, I'll pick something up from the grocery store. I'll be there soon."

An hour later he arrived at the front of the house honking. I saw him pull up and park. "Yvonne, go. Your father is waiting for you outside."

"But mom, why is he here? I don't want to go."

"I said go, Yvonne. He will be fine. Listen to me and go, please. Do it for me." I walked her to the door and helped her out the house. "Don't worry. He'll bring you back soon." I watched as she walked to him and then I saw her tear-filled eyes looking back at me.

"Wait, mom, I forgot to kiss you."

She ran back and kissed me on the cheek. I cringed at the thought of my once sweet baby, now capable of having her own child. Would she fall into every possible statistic of a single-parent household, of a daughter whose father was absent from her life? Now, my biggest fear was that Yvonne was going to be a lost youngster, looking for love in all the wrong places. What could be worse than that? Teenage pregnancy.

CHAPTER EIGHTEEN

Shortly after our divorce was finalized in April of 1980, Curtis' attorney filed a "stipulation for sale of real property." We would have to list the property for sale within a reasonable time. He was all in for putting the house up for sale, but I, according to the courts, obtained the use and possession denied by the judge because of what they referred to as my "intransigent behavior." What they failed to understand was that I had the right to fight for what was equally mine.

Two and half years later, I was still in the house raising my children. I refused to leave my home and Curtis wasn't going to make me do it. Whenever the judge reminded me to comply with the sale of the house, my response, which I didn't share aloud, was always, "over my dead body."

The sky, a grey watercolor pattern, was wet and dull. The whole town was changing, settling deeper in its roots, into the true experience of spring. It was now April 18, 1989, the azaleas had budded and the news all over the metropolitan area was the upcoming march in DC supporting Rowe v. Wade. Inside the home, I had finished cleaning the kitchen and prepared the children's after-school snacks. I took a seat at the dining room table, which was riddled with years of nicks, dents, and water rings and insisted on carrying out my daily routine as usual.

A month ago the court had denied my request for use and possession of the family home. Against my will, a trustee was appointed to manage and sell my house. I acted like I didn't hear my lawyer when he assured me, "upon the final sale, the proceeds would be equally divided between the two of you after all expenses were paid."

Through all the madness, Yvonne was now a sixth grader, a growing resilient young lady. From the outside, it didn't appear that the divorce or custody battle had affected her day-to-day life. I saw Yvonne as a typical youngster. She was on honor roll every quarter, a patrol monitor, considered a pleasant child to teachers and administration, and quickly made friends at school. I was proud of the sophisticated little lady she was growing up to be. Despite many difficulties posed by her father, I had made sure she was never absent or tardy. I always dropped her off and picked her up except on occasions where her father went against a court order and picked her up early from school instead of at the house. It was his way of getting me back for living in the house and refusing to put it up for sale. Now, I feared he would harm the children. Frequently I called the school to remind them of the court order which stated Curtis was not permitted to pick Yvonne up from school. More often than not, she ended up going with him anyway to prevent making a scene or the office would have difficulty keeping up with the ever-changing court orders.

As the school year progressed, I observed Yvonne's fascination with her teacher, Mr. Henry, who looked a lot like a thin Santa Claus. Like all other Pine Crest parents, I knew he was a favorite amongst sixth graders. Everybody loved him including my daughter. I couldn't deny he was a positive influence on Yvonne. It was clear by the enthusiasm from which she eagerly shared what she had learned at school: "Mommy, Guess what? Mr. Henry brought a Civil War gun to class today!" Or how he helped Yvonne master fractions after school or more recently how she won a trip to go fishing with him at a school fundraiser. Mr. Henry's compassion for my daughter was most evident when he paid for her to attend a field trip to the Liberty Bell. So overwhelmed with gratitude was I that it never dawned on me exactly how he knew I couldn't afford for her to attend. He went from being a teacher to advocate to a friend. And then I was confronted with facing one of my fears, Mr. Henry had evolved into the role of father figure.

My feelings were conflicted. Mr. Henry wasn't a bad role model and genuinely cared for my daughter. The problem was that Yvonne *had* a father, a man with serious issues. And now I had to watch my daughter search for ways to fill the hole in her heart. The excitement in her voice when she shared with me that she won the trip to go fishing was like a new child speaking. It was unusual for me to hear her exude so much excitement. Was her new happiness proof of how horrible things had been in our life? How was I going to create normalcy for my children? Oh, how I prayed God would keep them from being hurt beyond repair.

I lived in denial of the court planning to sell my home. With all the time that had passed since the initial threat, I imagined it wouldn't happen. Besides, the house was paying for itself. Curtis didn't have to pay a penny. Then I remembered all the money he needed to pay the lawyers from keeping him out of jail and the urge to suddenly vomit came upon me.

I piled all my documents and paperwork in front of me on the table including the latest unopened court correspondence from my attorney. Then I sighed and took on the perilous task of facing, opening, and reading a month's worth of unopened correspondence, cut off notices, and bills upon bills - all reminders that Curtis had stopped providing. The first envelope I had opened was from my attorney. Just looking at the letter made a fiery numbness spread like venom through my entire body and then I read:

Curtis and Nusrat have been unable to reach any agreement or be cooperative for several years. For three years, Curtis has kept all the rent from the investment apartments and has used them to defray his obligation of support. He denied Nusrat any share of the income from the premises while he had sufficient income to meet his own needs and to contribute the recommended amount to support his children.

Curtis owned General Electric stock for $17,000, which he acquired prior to meeting Nusrat in 1974. He said that he sold his Continental Telephone stock valued at $9,000 on his pre-trial statement to pay off his debt to his mother. That stock was acquired during their marriage.

Since the separation, Curtis has lived with his mother and insists "the rent from the two other apartments was not enough to pay all the expenses when lawn mowers and odds and ends were included." He also said that he used the funds from the sale of stocks purchased during the marriage to pay his attorney's fees and repay loans to his mother. The loans from his mother were the $300 per month that he said he was paying his mother in rent. He sold stock and gave his mother the check for the proceeds. He closed a joint account in early 1983 where there was at least $6000 in the jointly titled account. At one point Curtis collected rent of $880 per month from the rental units. Utility bills are approximately $275.00 per month. Curtis had not paid his mother any rent until he sold the Continental Telephone stock recently.

Beginning in Feb. 1983 Curtis started converting joint assets for his own use. Nusrat had a job as a secretary but quit the job at the end of the school year because the sitter for the children cost as much as she made. His financial statement presented to the court did not include his dividends on his General Electric Stock, $554 in 1984 or dividends from his Continental Telecom Inc. stock ($474 in 1984) now sold.

Curtis received income tax refunds for joint returns for years 1982, 1983, and 1984, all of which were filed in 1986. He received refunds of $1,051 and deposited the check without endorsement. The money went into a jointly titled property management account. All funds were entirely in his control where he used them for how he saw fit.

I paid for half of the property, had three children, and was denied all financial benefit. This was a painful reality to face when one had to set aside dignity to feed children and survive. By now, my blood boiled. He had a lot of nerve to say the money from the renters wasn't enough to fix everything *he* vandalized with his own *damned hands*. Where was the justice? For the past three years, I had been denied food stamps and other social services. The reason? It wouldn't make sense to give someone help if they owned a property that brought income. And that's what the documents show! Curtis *took* the money from the renters. Why couldn't the government see that?

Without the help of social services, I had to figure out how to live and survive. I borrowed here and there living at the mercy of people's generosity. I never imagined my life would've ended up like this. Instead of helping, the courts were hurting us by not enforcing the law. My three children were American and they had rights in this country, a fact I often reminded my lawyer. It's as if Curtis got away with murder. How was he able to get away with *not* paying child support for *his* three children? I'd be better off if I took them to Iran where I would at least have the help of family.

Similarly, the other letters seemed stale, flat, devoid of even a window of hope, and served as a constant source of stress. There was only one that stood out from the rest. The one that sat catty-corner to the edge of the rectangular table. Unlike the other letters, this one sat alone in the place it had fallen. I now recalled how I felt a sudden paralysis upon flipping to the last page. That's where the government seal mocked me with cherry red letters that read "DENIED."

From that point, I just left the letter there. I hadn't mustered the courage to reread the words. But then an odd sense to revisit the words came over me. I needed clarity as to why the court didn't feel my argument was valid. Not only was I denied, but the courts essentially usurped my position as co-owner to sell the house while we still lived in it. And to add insult to injury, I was forced to pay rent to the new owners who were hell-bent on displacing me out of my own damned home. The pain from looking at the pile of letters from my lawyers demanding me to vacate the property was killing me.

I vowed to the new owners and myself, to never give in to their threats of kicking me out. And to think they labeled me a "squatter." I never knew this word until now and it left a nasty taste in my mouth. It just didn't make sense to me when I knew that I had made a strong case. Didn't the court care that three American children would be sent to live on the street? Or was my Iranian origin a hindrance to the American promise? What about the words engraved on monuments, written in books, and broadcasted in foreign minds? *Give me your tired, your poor, your huddled masses yearning to be free...* Or were these just mere words that gave breath to generations of American men who would make it to the castle of liberty? Would the female foreigner be forever relegated to live under second-class begging for crumbs to feed America's forgotten children? I decided to reread the letter in search of something that I may have missed. Surely there was something that may have misguided the court's decision.

March 27, 1989
Dear Honorable Towner,

This letter serves to properly inform the court that I am being denied due process.

For three years, I have been bounced around a court system where no attorney would touch my case and a court system that refuses to hear my outcry. Having the qualification of a B.S. degree in History and a diploma in computer operating systems and working in the technology field, I certainly did not anticipate that I would end up being abused by a sick man and a court system that did not defend my rights.

The court-appointed trustee, Rachel S. Parks, notified me that on April 18, 1989, the Sheriff's Department would evict me and my three innocent children to justify a divorce settlement. After seven years of battery, mental and emotional abuse, and finally on Feb. 4, 1983, a loaded gun to my heart and threat to my life, I was left with no choice but to seek a divorce from Curtis Brown.

I have been indirectly victimized by lawsuits from tenants who refused to pay our rent. Mr. Brown has tried through various means to smear my name and character. He has crushed my credibility in the eyes of the public, law enforcement officials and the court system. I have not been given a chance by the court to accurately make my plight known. I feel that I have been systematically left defenseless. Six years of my life has been a battleground to protect my children and defend our rights.

It took three years of continuous struggle with Mr. Brown and the court system to finally get the divorce granted. It took another 21 months for the court to enforce child support and alimony, a mere total of $1000 for a family of four. I had to sustain my life with the help of a few charitable and conscientious friends during that time. How did Mr. Brown and the court system manage to get away with paying $187.50 to support a family of four from October 1983 through December 1987? This shows a lack of respect for human lives. Why doesn't the court system enforce its laws?

I've struggled to raise funds from friends to pay for electricity that had not been paid by Mr. Brown for five months ending Sept. 1987. From November 1987 until the present, Mr. Brown has failed to pay the gas, electricity, and water bills. To force the eviction of his three children and me when he has refused to pay the mortgage from November 1987 to November 1988 is outrageous. I had to pay the sum of $687.00 for a self-sufficient three-unit apartment house. From one end I received $1000 through the court, but from another end, $687.00 had to be paid for the mortgage and the sum of $200 for utilities so we could avoid being a liability to the state; trying to live off $100.00 a month for a family of four was impossible. It has been a constant struggle to keep the family's head above water not to mention how it becomes humiliating when one has to continually beg and ask for help.

I would like to bring to your attention a statue of law that indicates children under 21 years of age should live in a family home in the event of divorce to give them emotional stability. The law evidently does not apply to my children since they are scheduled to be evicted from their home on April 18, 1989 with no place to go.

The court has not supported me as the plaintiff, even with all the evidence I have presented. I feel the court was not fair in my case and if it becomes necessary to reopen the case, I am prepared to go through with it. I am pleading now; please do not disrupt our lives with an eviction. How can I raise three responsible children to become productive, law-abiding members of society when the court is not enforcing the statutes to protect them? How does Mr. Brown, with an annual salary of over $30,000 get away with neglecting his family thus far without going to jail? There are many cases of spouses going to jail for lack of child support. Why is he getting preferential treatment?

A citizen who has failed to provide as a father, who has abused his wife and children, and who has neglected his responsibility as a law-abiding citizen cannot be a positive role model for children or his place of employment or as a citizen of this country.

As a last resort, I am sharing my struggle with a few elected officials and private people with whom I have trust and confidence. I plead with you to look into this matter and assist me in any way you can. I do not want us to be a public liability. Please help in preventing the sale of our home and displacing a family of four.

Respectfully,
Nusrat Brown

Just as I finished reading the last line, loud knocks came from the front door. I went to see who was knocking so abruptly. Looking through the peephole, I didn't see anyone but then heard a voice.

"Mrs. Brown, this is Sheriff Hicks of the Montgomery County Sheriff's office. We are asking that you come out of the house."

"Oh Shit!" I looked through the peep-hole and saw him standing with his badge to the door. The reflection from the light made it difficult for me to see anything else. *Oh my God, what do I do?* My heart raced and horror set in. The tightening in my shoulders caused me to shift and adjust myself into an appropriate posture should they bang the door down. *Were they going to finally evict me and the children? I felt like I needed to call someone, but whom?* Everyone was at work. Then I went to the kitchen to call Curtis' mother. Before I could dial the third number, I heard a bang from the front door.

"Come out, Mrs. Brown."

"Over my dead body! You can't do this!"

I heard the officer ask for back up on his walkie-talkie.

"Mrs. Brown, we have a warrant to come into the home. You no longer own it and you are breaking the law."

"Breaking the law? I didn't agree to sell my home! *You* are breaking the law! Where am I supposed to go? I have three small children!"

"Mrs. Brown, we need you to open the door." A woman's voice said.

"Who are you?"

"I am Officer Morgan Ma'am. Please do not make this situation worse. It is going to happen today and we need you to comply."

I opened the door and over the next few hours, I watched as each item from my home was thrown on the front lawn. My clothes, the children's toys, my mattress, the pots and pans, my whole life! Everything I worked so hard for was now visible for all to see. Officer Morgan, the only woman there beside me, offered some advice before she left the property. "Fight for your kids. Do *not* let him win. You *fight* for them."

Fight? How was I supposed to fight? My lawyer couldn't stop this from happening. He merely delayed the inevitable. Can I trust that a lawyer could help me keep my children too?

I don't know how I took care of the children after the eviction. Several therapists and people at the mosque suggested that I give Darlene and Kevin to an Iranian Jewish family. But what would I do if something happened to them? I didn't want to give my children to anyone, not to a foster home, an Iranian family, to *nobody*. A Sister from the mosque told me that there was a doctor at Washington Adventist hospital who wanted to adopt a child since his wife was having difficulty conceiving. I just couldn't grasp why people had so much trouble accepting that even though my children were a burden, they were still *my* children. I told them all as plain as I could, "God gave me these children. I'm not giving them to *anyone*."

I knew Yvonne had witnessed the terrible things her father had done: the beatings, destruction of property, raping me and now all this. Lately, she was acting rebellious and a little disrespectful. The therapist suggested that this was a mere "acting out" similar to how he explained the behavior of the younger children. I was at ease knowing she had someone like Mr. Henry, a trusted adult in her corner.

I knew it was critical for her to have a positive experience with a male figure. I didn't want her to have a distorted image of men or have the belief that all men were abusive like her father. For this reason, I saw Mr. Henry as a God-sent gift.

Ending my life was never an option, but I had wondered how God could give me three children and put us in this situation. As of today, we had lived with eight different people in four months. What did I do to deserve this? I did what was right in the sight of God. I married and sacrificed my life for my children, so why was this all happening? My life had been one nightmare after another shooting by like fire-tipped darts to my chest.

It was a time I had to conceal from the school the fact that the kids were living in several places all over Maryland and DC. It was a time of survival, desperation, and deep humiliation. Where was the justice? How could the courts get away with not releasing my portion of the settlement? How could they just displace us? At times I felt like I was going crazy. Trying to make sense of it all, I sought clarity which only made me feel more burdened and overcome with grief. This was where I wanted to give up, but who would have taken care of my children?

Struggling to be a mother, let alone trying to be a father, I was relieved knowing Yvonne had someone outside the home to rely on in some way. I didn't feel like I had to ask her about every little detail of her school day. I knew who her friends were and didn't have a reason to be concerned about them. Mr. Henry was another set of eyes for me and this was comforting. But Yvonne would ultimately do something that I least expected: tell Mr. Henry everything that was *really* happening.

CHAPTER NINETEEN

But it was more than that. Ever since I walked in on my dad forcing himself on my mom, I changed. It wasn't something I could discuss in therapy. I wanted to save my mom and protect her from my dad. I had always seen more than my parents realized or wanted to admit. I kept most of it inside and sometimes I'd talk with my mom, but it would always make me sad. I knew my mom loved me which is why it hurt when she stopped hugging and kissing me. No, I wasn't a baby anymore, but wasn't I still *her baby*? I did whatever I could to help her around the house. It wasn't her fault that our life had been so tough. I just wished my dad loved us and cared about our lives more than he did his own.

My mom knew Mr. Henry was my favorite teacher in the whole wide world. He was always there to listen and help me with my problems. But it wasn't until the spring of my sixth-grade year where life, as I knew, would be changed forever.

It was a Monday morning and my mom called the school reminding them that my dad was not permitted to pick me up. But like so many times before, he arrived half an hour before dismissal. Over the inter-com the secretary said, "Please pardon the interruption, Mr. Henry, can you please send Yvonne Brown to the office for early dismissal?"

"Yes, she'll be right there." He looked at me and my eyes grew wide with fear.

Today, I refused to go outside with him and stayed in the classroom. "He's not supposed to be here." I looked at the clock. There were five minutes to the bell. Fidgeting with my hands, I felt dried glue on my finger from cutting and pasting images of Greek gods. "I'm afraid that if I go with him that he'll hurt me."

"Don't worry. No one's going to hurt you."

For a moment I felt like Mr. Henry was Superman coming to my rescue and then I saw my father at the class door. *Oh my God!* Searching for an escape, I saw the orange poster board which read *Wall of Excellence* taped over the door. The smell of microwave popcorn lingered into the classroom from the teacher next door. I felt like I wanted to vomit. I saw the emergency side door at the back of the classroom and decided that would be my exit. As I crept towards the door, I noticed Mr. Henry went to the classroom door. "Please be careful. He's crazy." I prayed he would say or do something to make my father leave peacefully. All I could make out from their talk was that my dad said, "We can take this outside buddy."

"Oh my God! Dad no! Leave! Just leave!"

"Don't worry Yvonne, it's going to be okay." Mr. Henry stepped out into the hallway. A few minutes later, he returned a little mad. "See, I told you everything would be okay. I'm taking you home."

"What do you mean? Where did he go?"

"Not sure, but I know that he will not be picking you up anymore from school."

For the first time, I felt protected and safe. How could I express my gratitude? The next day Mr. Henry introduced a new journal assignment. He told us to fold a sheet of paper in half. On one side we were to write about whatever we wanted. The fold down the middle separated who was speaking and was usually headed with a date and a "Dear Mr. Henry" or "Dear Yvonne." In turn, he promised to respond to each of us individually. I was excited because I had so much to share. I couldn't wait to write about attending a Capitol's hockey game, what I ate or the arguments between me and my best friend, Diana.

I really wanted to be a "normal kid" who came from a "normal family." There were questions I had for Mr. Henry that I couldn't bring myself to ask. I wanted answers to why was my family so messed up? Why did my mother now wish we were dead? Eventually, I built the courage to open up. I thought it was because Mr. Henry didn't respond to me like I was an immature 11-year-old girl. It was like he really cared. I loved the assignment so much that I thought I'd keep all my papers in a safe place for the rest of my life.

March 9, 1989
Dear Mr. Henry,

Yesterday someone told me that I was the type of person that likes getting my way. Do you think that I'm that type of person?

Sincerely,
Yvonne

March 10, 1989
Dear Yvonne,

I think there is probably a little of that in all of us. We each want our own way in things. It's human nature. You may not like it, but take a step back and see if it's true. If it is, then work on it. If it's not, then smile.

Sincerely,
Mr. Henry

March 13, 1989

Dear Mr. Henry,

I miss Diana very much. She's the only friend I've ever had at this school. I'm mad that she hasn't called. I don't know her number and I've tried my best to get it from her father. Wherever she is, I would like to move in. I think she hasn't called because of her mom. Maybe her mom found out about her sharing too much?

Sincerely,

Yvonne

My hair was brown and super thick. Kids teased me for having "bushy" hair and "boats" for feet. It didn't help that my loafers made my size 8 feet look larger. Perhaps I could've used a little hair gel or conditioner, but my mother didn't bother herself with things like that. Then one day I came to school with a new hairstyle. Mr. Henry complimented my new look as I entered the classroom. I responded with a respectful "Thank you," but I was heartbroken and couldn't wait to write and tell him all about it:

March 14, 1989

Dear Mr. Henry,

My dad got my hair done. He took me to a salon in Chevy Chase. My hairdresser washed my hair and said, "Wow, your hair has grown all the way down the middle of your back!" I didn't see the scissors in her hand. I didn't see the ponytail she formed or the big cut she made close to my head. I just felt the air from the fan around my neck and heard one big "snip" of the scissors. I was shocked. All she could say was, "Sorry Hon, I know it hurts, but that's what your dad wanted." It was his weekend and he tricked me. He said it was punishment for my grades, but my grades are good. What does he expect? My parents are in and out of court!

Sincerely,

Yvonne

After a couple of weeks, the letters changed. It was like Mr. Henry became the dad I had always hoped for in my life. I felt more comfortable with talking about my parent's divorce. Whether I read the letters in class or after school in a hotel, I clung to every word.

March 28, 1989
Dear Mr. Henry,

I feel like Diana and I are going through the same thing. It kills me that her mother won't let me talk to her. I need her to know what's happening now since my parents are fighting over custody. She's the main one that understands what I'm going through. I might be permanently staying with my dad. Before that could happen, I would run away or do something worse.

Sincerely,
Yvonne

March 29, 1989
Dear Mr. Henry,

I don't believe that I'm going to move. I think I'm going to let my father down since he's making plans for us to live with him. When we stayed with him last weekend, he showed us the school that we would be going to next year. He just wants things to work out in his favor. This makes me blue. Sometimes I sit in my bedroom and talk to Bridgette, my Cabbage Patch Kid. She's adorable. She has curly red hair and she's washable. My dad gave her to me as a Christmas gift last year.

Sincerely,
Yvonne

March 30, 1989

Dear Yvonne,

It must be hard for you especially since you are torn between two parents and you love them both. I know that it may be easy to say, but I know it will work out. Things seem to be falling apart around you. You must be strong. This is a time for you to lean on your friends for support. Always remember that there are people who love you. I know that I can't offer much nor can I pretend that I have the power to change things. All I have to offer is my friendship when you are in need.

This is a bad day for me. I have some not so good news of my own. Diana knows, but I've asked her not to share it with anyone. I think I need to tell you, as well. Please keep it between the two of you. On Monday when I was absent, I found out that I need an operation on my eyes and quick. There's always a catch isn't there?

There is a possibility that I can become permanently blind. I don't mean to scare you, but I'm going to fly to Florida next Friday to get it all done. It is important that I share with you some things before the weekend begins. I may not see you again after today. There may be a new teacher when you come back to school.

Even though I am gone from here, it won't mean that I've forgotten you or that I will not still worry about your well-being. There's hope for me and there is hope for you too. I will give you my phone number and address so that we can keep in touch.

You are a good person. Don't ever give up.

Your friend and teacher,
Mr. Henry

March 31, 1989
Dear Mr. Henry,

I will probably finish out this year. Yesterday my mom said that I would be going to Sligo Middle School. By the way, I pray for you every night. I see you have the patch on your eye again. Are your eyes okay?

Sincerely,
Yvonne

April 3, 1989
Dear Yvonne,

I don't quite get why you have to move. Maybe talking about it will help. I am going to be on recess duty today if you would like to talk. I know it is rough, but it's not the end of the world. I can't tell you what the future may bring for you, but I do know that you have to be strong. That's lousy advice, isn't it? That's the worst part of teaching. I'll miss you.

Mr. Henry

April 10, 1989
Dear Yvonne,

I did not have my operation. I went to Florida, but the doctor got sick himself. I'll wait until school is over if I can. Thank you for your card and prayers.

Mr. Henry

April 11, 1989
Dear Mr. Henry,

I will be moving on April 15th which is three days before my 12th birthday. My parents had a nasty fight over our home. You see, my parents own a garden apartment. We live in the middle apartment and my parents rent out the top and bottom apartments. I'm sure you have figured out that my parents are divorced. They do not get along, so my father is selling our house. I don't love him. I am in a big mess!

Sincerely
Yvonne

April 12, 1989
Dear Mr. Henry,

Everything is going fine so far especially since my wish came true. Nobody came to dump our furniture out as my mother thought. Can you believe I'm going to be 12 years old? I just hope it doesn't happen tomorrow. Meaning, the police carrying out our furniture like they almost did last week after school. I don't think it's normal for a sixth grader to go through all this stuff.

Sincerely,
Yvonne

April 13, 1989
Dear Yvonne,

I know it is hard for you to believe you're going to move. This is how I look at it. I may be right or wrong. Your father wants both you and him to be happy. Isn't it very possible that even though you have had some hard times that your father loves you? This is not to say he is doing the right thing to you and for you. Maybe he feels like he is doing what is correct. My hope is that you will still be going to this school. Do you know that I pray for you?

Mr. Henry

April 19, 1989

Dear Mr. Henry,

Yesterday at ten o'clock in the morning the sheriff and the police finally evicted us because my father wanted to get his share of the house immediately. They threw out all of our furniture and personal items. My Cabbage Patch Kid was thrown on the curb. I wiped the dirt off her face.

I do not have a house anymore. I can't believe I am writing this down. The people that bought our home live in the downstairs apartment. They threatened to get my mother arrested if she did not get off "their property" immediately. My little brother cussed them out and my sister kicked one of the officers.

I'm sorry that I seem to make you sad with my life. I won't talk about it anymore. Is your big operation happening soon?

Sincerely,

Yvonne

April 20, 1989

Dear Mr. Henry,

We do not have a telephone at the hotel we are temporarily living. Thank you for admiring my strength. This is a scary place. I hope we can return home soon.

Sincerely,

Yvonne

I was late to school a lot. My mother had difficulty getting me there since the hotel was so far away. I wondered if Mr. Henry wondered why I wasn't in school and if he was worried about me. After three days, my mom was able to get me there. Once again, I was happy to be seated at my desk. As he did every morning, Mr. Henry collected the class notes and gave the next assignment. Before I started, I noticed him searching through the letters and prayed he was looking for mine to read first.

April 24, 1989
Dear Mr. Henry,

Guess what my father knows? He knows where we're staying and my mom is worried that he will take us away from her. He accused my mother of making us stay up late to make her seem like a bad person. He asked the judge if he could have custody of us this week. The judge honored his wish. That makes me so mad. I will never forget what he has done to us in the past and for what he has done to my mother.

I know he thinks that I was too young to remember it all, but I do. Will the judge see that he is not a good father? Did the judge examine all of the court documents that prove he is hurtful? He must know my father is not a good person. Remember when you asked me why and how my father gets away with all of it? My mom says it is because he gets along with the "system." I think she might be right.

Sincerely,
Yvonne

April 25, 1989
Dear Yvonne,

Your father is probably broke. The judge must feel that your father has some rights to you even though it is little. Have you given some thought to not answering the phone? I'm afraid you're not going to get a perfect world. At least this is better than the ideas you had before having to go away and live with him.

Mr. Henry

April 26, 1989

Dear Mr. Henry,

I am living at my aunt's house now. She's not my real aunt, but she's the first person that my mom met when she came to America. Out of respect, my mom told us that we have to call her Auntie. I guess this living situation is better than staying in a hotel. Lucky for me, she has a cute dog named Mr. Scott and it is my job to walk him every day.

Sincerely,
Yvonne

April 27, 1989

Dear Mr. Henry,

Let me tell you about the exciting episode that happened yesterday. When I got to my aunt's house, my father came and said he wanted to take me and I refused. He threatened me with the police. I said in my mind "fine." Then my mom's lawyer called and told me to listen to my father and go with him. I listened and when I went to his van, he refused me.

Sincerely,
Yvonne

April 28, 1989

Dear Yvonne,

Thank you so much for your thoughtful card. It was kind of you to think of me.

Your father is putting a lot of effort and money into having you in his life. Apparently, this shows that he must care. Does it matter to you if your father loves you? It sounds as though he does. I have heard you express the opposite about him.

Can you expect love without giving it? Is that what you want?
Even though I happen to agree with you about what's happening now, there are always two sides to everything. I'm just sad
that people have to do this mess to each other and then call
it love.

Sincerely,
Mr. Henry

It was hard for me to think of good memories with my father. I wanted to forget about the beatings and all of the things he had destroyed. I
wished that I had a good memory of him. It's like whatever good he may
do for me was only because the courts made him do it. I wanted to trust
him, but I just couldn't bring myself to that point.

May 1, 1989
Dear Mr. Henry,
    I think I put it in the wrong way. I know he loves me and I
love him as well. What I'm trying to say is that he doesn't care. He
only buys us clothing or shoes when a court hearing is around
the corner. I hate to say it, but it looks like he wants to look good
for court. I can't wait for this to end so I can finally have my own
bedroom.

Sincerely,
Yvonne

May 2, 1989
Dear Mr. Henry,
    I found out that my father did call the police. Luckily they
were on my mother's side. Today my mom will go with an inspector to see the house we might be getting. For some reason, I don't

think my father loves me anymore. I think he just wants to have custody to do something terrible, mean, and painful to me.

Sincerely,
Yvonne

May 3, 1989
Dear Mr. Henry,

Can a man be broke when he has a lot of hundred-dollar bills in his wallet and eats Chinese food all the time? Tomorrow, I will not be in school. I am going to court to testify against my father. It's because he busted my mother's headlights and I think it's for beating me too. Yesterday my mom went to court for custody. I wrote a letter to the judge requesting to live with my mom. At first the judge hesitated to read it, but in the end, my mom won custody of me!

Sincerely,
Yvonne

May 4, 1989
Dear Yvonne,

Maybe he is broke. I knew you would win.

Mr. Henry

May 8, 1989
Dear Mr. Henry,

Today we are expecting to go to our new home! I've planned everything for my room. I know what my chores are going to be and how much allowance my mother will give me. I can't wait for us to settle down and be away from my dad. His best accomplishment was making me, my brother, and sister.

Next weekend he wants us to be with him for two weeks! There is no way, no how, that I am going to miss going to my house. He tells me that I am living like a gypsy. I remember one time he called me and this is what he said, "Honey, I am going through much more than you."

Yeah right! Last night I had a nightmare that he told me in a calm voice, "Yvonne, honey, sit here. Daddy is going to kill you." It scared me to death. It seemed so real.

Right now I'm eating a delicious chocolate éclair and watching "I Dream of Genie." I'm here alone in the hotel room wishing I could blink myself out of all my problems.

Sincerely,
Yvonne

May 9, 1989
Dear Yvonne,

I know we communicate only through these letters and you may feel that you can't talk to me as a friend. I may seem nosy to you, but it's just that I want to know how you are handling things. If it's better for me to shut my mouth, then I will. Also, you don't make me sad. Talk about it all you need to. That's what friends are for.

Mr. Henry

May 10, 1989
Dear Mr. Henry,

You are not nosy. I don't mind sharing my pain. I need someone to tell what's going on in my life. After all, you have been like a father to me. My mother said that she would take care of the money for the field trip to the aquarium. I know you are nice, but I just don't feel right with you offering to pay my way.

But, if my mom can't pay for it, I will take you up on your offer. Thank you. What happened yesterday? My dad took me to Bob's Big Boys. Then we went to Sears and then we went to my sister's psychiatrist appointment. For some reason, I also ended up in her session. The psychiatrist asked me how I felt about my parent's divorce and I said I didn't care because I know my father is abusive.

Sincerely,
Yvonne

June 9, 1989
Dear Yvonne,

I have given some thought to writing you this letter. It may not mean anything to you now, but I hope that you will keep it for a while in hopes that it will have more meaning for you in the future.

You've been through a lot this school year and none of it has been easy. Sometimes things have to be worse before they can get better. One goes along in life thinking that everything is fine and then suddenly things fall apart. I wish that life were not so complicated, but we all have obstacles to face and emotions to handle.

You've done great. I know you have the strength to keep on pushing. As long as you have been my student, I have waited for you to share your problems instead of asking questions that would hurt you as you're dealing with things.

You may consider me an old man, but I too understand pain and disappointment. Life has not treated you kindly, that much is clear. The thought of you moving on like this makes me feel like I am casting you back into the world with now only my prayers and unfinished work. No, I can't feel in the same way you do at your age, but I can understand.

Don't hate anyone. Easy to say, however, it is hard to do. Life is too short to hate anyone or anything. When you hate, it destroys your insides and that kind of damage can never be undone.

More advice? Make friends. Keep them. Most importantly, tell them that you love and care for them. That's the kind of thing that people don't do enough. Like you, I am a survivor. Thinking of my operation makes me depressed sometimes, but I'll make it or die trying. Last of all, believe in yourself. Thank you for being a friend. I will always be here for you.

Love,
Tom Henry

CHAPTER TWENTY

On May 4, 1989, I walked up the steps of the Rockville courthouse for an emergency court hearing with my mother. My brother and sister were in school and too young to share their experiences in court. I couldn't believe that for the first time, a hearing was called as a result of what my father had done to me. It was all so unreal. But as I watched my mother check in with the clerk who looked at my visible injuries, I knew that some line no longer invisible had been crossed.

From the bench in the waiting room, I sat dreading what the outcome was going to be. Would I have to live with my father? Would he finally go to jail for refusing to pay child support? Would the judge believe his desperate, vicious lies about my mother being unfit? Would the judge accept my testimony? What would the judge think about our living situation? With so much uncertainty, the weight of not knowing what would happen next was just too much.

The waiting room with its dark brown wooden furniture and floors made me sad. I'd been here for countless other reasons relating to my parents' divorce. Waiting for my case to be called, I prayed I wouldn't have to see my father's face or fight the urge to spit at him. It was

8:00 a.m. and more people entered the room to wait for their case number. Then, in walked a kid with whom I perceived were his parents and lawyer. Watching him take a seat directly across from where I was sitting, I gathered we were close in age.

He wore baggy jeans, a freshly ironed white t-shirt, and had his starter jacket folded over his lap. Because of his skin color, he would've been the kind of guy my father disapproved of for dating. As he took a seat between the two adults, I whispered in my mother's ear, "I think he's cute."

"*Cute?*"

I could tell she was controlling her voice from rising.

"We're sitting here waiting for our court hearing and you're talking about a boy being *cute?*"

Well, there was nothing else to do, but think about things and he *was* cute. I thought I was pointing out the obvious. It wasn't a big deal. But to my mother, anything about boys was always a big deal. I just wished she didn't think I wanted to have sex with him because I said he was cute. Gosh, I couldn't keep my eyes off of him. Was his family in a custody battle too? Was his father abusive to him and his mother? I was curious and created possible scenarios in my mind as to why he was also in court.

I watched him as he carefully maneuvered his hand from underneath his coat to scratch his face. It was then that I caught a glance of the handcuffs hidden under his jacket. And like a person mesmerized by a dancing snake, I fixed my eyes on him so intently that finally, his eyes met mine just seconds before my case was called.

"Yvonne!" My mother pinched my arm. "Don't you see the fire in my eyes? Get a hold of yourself. Our name has been called. Let's go!"

Entering the courtroom, I saw my father for the first time since the most recent incident. All the raw anger flushed over me as I fought back the tears. *No*, I thought. *I won't give him the pleasure of seeing me cry.* I wiped away the tears.

I had a hard time paying attention to the details of the hearing because images from the beating brought a tide of emotions. I heard the judge state that we were there for a review of custody due to alleged abuse. Then I saw my mother take the stand. During her account of what happened, I saw the deep lines beginning to form around her eyes and mouth. She was still beautiful, but her face looked like she hadn't slept for years. I focused on the details of her appearance so I wouldn't have to hear what was being said.

Finally, I was called to testify. As I took the stand, my eyes glanced at my father. His stare was even and cold. I quickly looked away. But I felt more confident and composed as any emotional connection I'd ever had with him was now buried under my hatred for what he had put me through. As I reached the stand and was sworn in, I knew that I had to tell exactly what had happened. It was the only way to get him out of my life forever.

"Yvonne, can you tell us in your own words what happened when you last visited your father?" The judge asked.

"Yes, Your Honor," I replied and began to recount the scene that I could never forget. And while it all happened a month ago, it felt like it happened just yesterday.

"It was a Friday evening around six o'clock. It had just finished raining when I looked out of the hotel window and saw my father's burgundy Suburban parked in front of the hotel. I then told my mom that he showed up. My brother and sister really wanted to see him, but I begged my mother not to make us go. She told me, 'I know you don't want to go with him, but it's a court order for you to go for the weekend.'

My gut told me that we shouldn't have gone with him, but I put my shoes on and packed up anyway. With all the moving we did, it was hard for him to keep track of us. This brought relief, but then it scared me how he eventually found out where we were staying. It was two weeks since we last saw him and spending time with him again made me nervous. He called the hotel room and I answered. I asked him if we could wash our clothes at our grandmother's house, where he was staying, where we always went when we visited him."

"Are you saying that you stayed at your grandmother's house with your father?"

"No, Your Honor. He picked up my grandmother and we all stayed in Virginia, at his new girlfriend's house. I knew something was seriously wrong when Sunday came and there was no discussion of him returning us home to our mother. The following day, our grandmother watched us while my dad and his girlfriend were at work. My father unplugged all the telephones except for the one next to my grandmother. She had the only working phone to use just in case she had to report something to my father. It was then that I realized he had kidnapped us and I had to make a plan to escape. I feared that I would never see my mother again and that my father had plans to do something bad to us. For my plan to succeed, I had to share it with my brother and sister. The plan was to tell our grandmother that we were going outside to play and instead of playing we were going to walk about a mile to 7-Eleven where I would call my mother from a pay phone to tell her where we were."

"And were you able to contact your mother?"

"Yes, Your Honor, everything went as planned. I told my mother where we were and she told us to go back and that she would get us as fast as she could. But when we got back, my little brother got in trouble with my grandmother for talking back. Before I knew it, he told my grandmother how we contacted our mother and everything went downhill from there. My grandmother turned to me and said, 'Is that right?' And then she called my father and told him everything. Then she made all three of us sit on the floor facing the front door. When our father came home from work, we were already positioned to tell him the truth. I was scared at the thought of him turning the lock, opening the door, and seeing us sitting there in our t-shirts and underwear. Finally, he came home and opened the door. His leather belt was already in hand. He demanded that I tell him what I had done, but I was too scared to speak. He told me that he already knew the truth and wanted to know if I contacted my mother. Then he cracked his belt, preparing to beat me. I moved back slowly, telling him that I wanted my mother."

"Yvonne, did your father hit you with the belt or only make sounds with it?"

"He struck me several times with the belt. I looked down and saw the buckle had busted a vein in my hand. I was so frightened and believed he wanted to kill me. I screamed, hoping a stranger from outside would help. I managed to kick him in his privates, then I immediately ran out the front door, forgetting I was not fully dressed. I was running for my life. I ran several blocks until I looked behind me and saw his Suburban preparing to corner me in an ally. It wasn't long before he grabbed me, threw me in the back of the truck, returned to his girlfriend's house, and beat me for what seemed like hours."

"To clarify Yvonne, did your father beat you for hours or did it just feel that way?"

"Well, the sun was out when he started and he didn't stop until bedtime."

"Can you describe what he did to you?"

"Yes, over and over again his belt landed on my body. On my arms, then my back, then my bottom, then my legs, then my back again. Several times he slapped me across the face whenever I jerked away from him, desperately trying to avoid each blow. I didn't know it was possible for mucus to come from my mouth from all the screaming. I remember that I had to spit up constantly. The entire time, my grandmother sat and watched like she was enjoying a movie. My brother and sister were crying and begging him to stop. When his girlfriend came home, my father invited her to beat me with the belt because he complained about his hand hurting. They beat me until they were both tired, then made me stand in the corner with my forehead faced into the wall for hours before I was allowed to sleep. If I was not facing the wall when they checked on me, then he said he would beat me all over again. I didn't move."

"What is the girlfriend's name?"

"Linda Batten."

"Is she here today?"

"No, Your Honor, she isn't here."

"Alright, continue."

"But at that point, I wasn't able to close my eyes because of the swelling. All I could do was pray my mother would be able to find us and come to our rescue. The next day, I had black and purple bruises all over me. My face was swollen, my body bruised, and there were cuts throughout my body from where the belt buckle hit. While my dad was at work, my mom picked us up. She called the police to report what my father had done to me, and now we are here."

"Thank you, Yvonne." The judge said. "Is there anything else you would like to add?"

"I just wanted to see my mother, Your Honor. If he loved me so much, would he beat me like this?" I asked, pointing to the remaining bruises on my face. "I know he's my father, but I don't want to live with him and I don't want to see him anymore."

"Thank you, Yvonne. You are very brave. You can go sit with your mother now."

The judge spoke gently to me as if to a small child. I could only nod slightly, then I walked back to my seat.

"Mr. Brown, I am shocked and appalled by your behavior. Not only do I *not* see fit for you to have continued custody of these children, but you are fortunate that criminal charges are not being pursued. If I had my way, you would be held accountable for your actions against your daughter to the full extent of the law. As it is, my role here concerns only custody and visitation between you and the children. So I am ordering your custody be terminated immediately and that any visitation between you and the children be supervised through the Department of Social Services. If you make any attempt to contact your children outside of meetings set up and supervised by the Department of Social Services, all visitation rights will be revoked. Furthermore, I will advocate for the County Attorney's office to revisit criminal charges for kidnapping and assault. Do I make myself clear?"

"Yes, ma'am," he responded with a smirk.

Listening to everything the judge had said to my father, I was in utter disbelief. I hadn't expected him to lose visitation. Finally, someone in authority saw past his mask and called him out on being the monster he really was in private. As my mother and I left the courthouse, I breathed a sigh of relief. I couldn't believe after everything I'd seen my father do to my mother, that a judge had finally taken action to stop the abuse. I looked at my mother hoping to see relief in her eyes too, but all I saw was a deep emptiness that seemed to be filling her from the inside out.

"Mom, is there any luck in finding a home yet?"

"Not sure. But we'll see."

CHAPTER TWENTY-ONE

I t was the end of July 1989 and we were staying with a Muslim doctor for a month. He offered his second home to us when he heard of our unfortunate situation. I've prayed this was our last temporary home and that my share from the sale of the house would come soon. This was no way to live.

I must confess, even in this challenging time, it was amazing to see there were still good-natured people in the world. The doctor and his wife gave us full use of their house including the spacious kitchen. Honestly, I enjoyed cooking again and preparing hot meals. I was delighted when I went to feed the children leftovers and saw the doctor and his wife had beaten me to it. From this moment, I took every opportunity I could to cook and leave food for them, it was the least I could do.

But this joy would be short-lived. The nights were unbearable: finding ways to settle the children and create a sense of stability was almost impossible. It was really something when the doctor went to court to question why the money had yet to be released. As long as I didn't have it, Curtis would use our living conditions as a reason to prove I was an unfit mother. Did it dawn on him that he was the one who had caused our life to be in misery? I didn't want to lose my children, but what was I going to do in the meantime? I couldn't just keep putting out Curtis' fires. I had to prove that I was doing everything humanly possible to keep my children. As crazy as it sounded, I decided to search for a home without a dime to my name.

My search began in places like Germantown and Gaithersburg. But, as soon as I went into those neighborhoods, I suddenly got unexplainably scared. So I narrowed my search to familiar areas near the Holy Cross Hospital and close to the mosque.

One morning while the children were staying with a friend, I drove near the hospital to check out possible homes. It was the first area I had thought of to explore seriously. It wasn't long before I stumbled upon a beautiful home with a promising "For Sale" sign. It was set in a well-kept lawn, just like all the other homes. Pink and white azalea bushes sprung from the entrance outlying the entryway. In no way did the home or neighborhood remind me of Garland Avenue. The houses looked like real homes, not garden apartments posing as homes. Each one had a driveway and a bay window.

I parked and asked Allah for a sign, whether this would be my house or not. Then I saw the address number 8201, the same address number for Garland Avenue. Wow! Allah works fast!

I walked to the backyard and saw enough space for the children to run, play, and make mud pies if they wanted. Smiling at the thought, I glanced at the shadows of the trees, which lingered over my head. Pulling out my notepad, I wrote down the address and info off the sign. At my first chance, I called my real estate agent and friend, Fati, who knew my situation. She was preparing for vacation with her husband, so she referred me to two ladies she trusted with Coldwell and Banker, Mrs. Perez and Mrs. Ali. Fati urged me to call them and that they would take care of me with what I needed.

Just like she promised, the ladies met me in no time to show the house. When I first entered the living room from the front door, I thought, "This was it. This was where we were supposed to live." Each of the four levels impressed me, but the sunroom and the kids having their own rooms and bathroom made it perfect. When the realtors asked me if I liked the home and if I saw my family living in it, I quickly responded *yes* and they immediately wrote up a contract—which required a $3,000 deposit.

Fati, may Allah bless her, paid for it. When she returned from vacation, her words put me at ease. "I know your share of the settlement is coming. I'm only doing for you what I would want someone to do for me if I was in your situation. I know your family is back home, which is why it would be a sin if I had the means to assist you and didn't."

By September, I had to purchase the house or the contract would be canceled. With the money in the court's hands and the deadline approaching, there was no sign of the money being disbursed. Now I was at risk of losing my contract on the house and being out of $3,000. But again, the real estate agents stepped in like angels and renewed it on faith. Months had passed, and the courts still didn't release the funds. I couldn't find the words to describe what it was like to be at the mercy of others. So much of what I had desperately needed depended on the decisions and availability of other people. With everything to lose, I wrote another letter. This time, it was addressed to the Attorney General. I prayed for a miracle.

The Honorable J. Joseph Curran, Jr.
Attorney General
State of Maryland

August 28, 1989
Dear Mr. Curran,

I am writing to you not only because of your position as State Attorney General but also because I understand that as a family man, you are compassionate and understanding.

I am concerned about the delay in disbursements of funds from the court ordered sale of my home, which took place on

April 18, 1989. Presently, I am represented by Attorney Roger McFee of Smith, Calhoun, and Alexander in Rockville, Md. Attorney Sonia Lacey is the court-appointed trustee and Judge Donald Ridge is presiding over this matter.

On July 13, 1989, I was informed by Attorney McFee that there were no further claims and that the claim period had expired. Thus, funds were to be released to me from the sale of the marital house. Since then, the funds have not been released and I have not been able to obtain a resolution.

Also, anytime that I can speak to my attorney and attorney Lacey, I am told a series of confusing and contradictory statements which frankly have led me to believe neither Attorney McFee nor Attorney Lacey are following the mandate of the courts. For example, in early August, Attorney McFee stated that the funds were going to be released immediately. Then he had a "pre-planned vacation" and stated he would take care of everything the week of August 21st. I spoke with him on the day he returned and he told me that "everything was fine with the funds," but he would have to file a motion against Attorney Lacey (trustee) and my former husband.

Of course, I believed what he was telling me only to find out on Friday, August 25th that he had given entirely different information about this matter to someone else. In fact, he stated to two other persons, that the funds were not going to be released in August, but that he would have to litigate my case again.

I am incredibly concerned about this matter for many reasons. I am a single mother with three children. The continued promises and delays caused by the lawyers and the legal system have prevented me from offering a stable home environment that my children need and deserve.

With these continued delays and lack of resolution, I fear that I will lose my children. I am, my children can tell you, a good mother, who unfortunately had to face a bitter divorce.

Now, all four of us are victims of domestic violence at the hands of my ex-husband. I beg you to assist my children and me by looking into this matter, and by doing what is in your power to bring it to closure.

Frankly, I don't know where to turn anymore. Friends that I know have worked with you in the past, such as members of the Latino community and other ethnic communities here in Montgomery County have told me repeatedly that you are the right source of help to end my unfortunate situation. I thank you for your time and eagerly await your response.

Sincerely,
Nusrat Brown

Four months after I was evicted from my house, the two real estate agents went to court and threatened the judge: "If you do not release the monies for this family to live in their own home, we are going to take this case to the media."

A month later, the courts had paid all the lawyers, legal fees, and I received my share. The world had been lifted from my shoulders as I signed the contract to close on our new home. Hopefully, this would be the last move – ever.

CHAPTER TWENTY-TWO

It was the last Friday of the summer and a new school year was about to begin. I had outgrown most of my skirts and pants. I had three pairs of jeans that were feeling a little tight and I needed a new pair of tennis shoes. My mom promised me that she would take me back-to-school shopping once she could. Not only was I going to attend a new school, but we were moving into our *new* home. I mean, it was really happening. No one would ever know how much I dreamed of decorating my walls with New Kids On the Block posters, placing stuffed animals on my bed and making new friends to invite over. My life was about to be perfect.

My mother hired two men to pick up our furniture from a storage unit all the way in Rockville. Following behind the moving truck, she told me that she was scared someone stole our belongings. Thankfully, everything was there the way she had left it. After the movers loaded the truck, we continued to follow them. When my mother pulled into the driveway, I felt jittery inside. We were home!

I couldn't believe how big it was compared to our old place. I counted three separate floors. My mom hadn't told us too much about it, I guess she didn't want to get our hopes up, but it *was* nice. Though it became dark outside, I could still see how the grass hadn't been cut in a while. But that didn't matter. We were no longer homeless, no longer living from suitcase to plastic bag, and no longer having to worry about being too loud for fear of getting kicked out of somewhere. Most importantly, we no longer had to worry about my dad coming to a place he didn't own.

Still in the car, I stared at the house and contemplated where my room was going to be and which part of the house it was going to face. I knew the largest bedroom in the house would go to my mom, which meant the second largest room was mine. How many closets would I have? How many windows? Finally, I could have a normal life just like the Cosby kids, who had chores and earned allowance for keeping their bedrooms clean (things I had dreamed about).

My mother got out of the car to open the house for the movers. My brother and sister jumped out and raced to the front door. I remained in the car taking in the full moment. This felt too perfect. Something terrible was bound to happen. I watched her try the key and pushed the door to open, but it wouldn't budge. *I knew it.* My stomach dropped. I went to see what was the problem.

"Oh my God! It's not working."

"Maybe it's the wrong key," I said. "Check to see if there's another key on your keychain."

"No, it's the right key. The other key is my car key." She said while jiggling the key up and down in the keyhole.

"Ma'am," one of the movers said. "Do you mind if I try? Let me help you."

My mother handed him the keys. She watched his hand as he turned the key. At last, he enforced power with his knee and the door opened.

"Whew!" He laughed. "But we got it open."

"Oh, thank you so much." My mom said. "I see, I have to push the door when I turn the key."

Darlene and Kevin rushed passed me to get into the house. I must have been nervous because my chest felt weird. I walked through the front door, looked into the living room on my left and the kitchen straight ahead. Then my eyes turned to the right and gazed at the five steps that would lead to my bedroom. Just as I took the first step to go upstairs, my mother yelled, "Yvonne!" Her voice was magnified by the echo in the empty house. "Don't go upstairs! Get out of the house, so the movers have space to bring in your furniture."

"But Mom, I haven't even seen my room."

"Don't worry, you'll have enough time to see it. Where's your brother and sister?"

"I don't know. Probably looking in the rooms or running around in the basement."

I returned to the car and sat while the furniture was being unloaded. I waited for everything to be moved in so nothing else would ruin my mother's moment. When the movers were ready to leave, the one who had helped get the door open tapped the car window to get my attention and said, "We're finished here, enjoy your new home!"

"Thank you." I smiled and went back to the house. I drowned out the noise of my brother and sister chasing each other through the rooms. I ignored the sound of my mother yelling at them to stop running and fighting. As usual, they didn't listen. This was going to be the first time that I didn't have to make them behave. This was going to be the first time that I had my own bedroom without a bunk bed. I had visions of my sanctuary away from my siblings and away from my mother when I needed a break. Nothing, and I mean nothing, was going to ruin this moment.

Entering the upstairs floor, I opened the door to each room. Which one was going to be mine? I entered the second largest room in the house and was surprised to see a walk-in closet and two big windows that faced the front of the house. I took a seat on one of the two twin beds in the room when my mother came to me and said, "You know this is not your room, right?"

"Why mom?" I started to cry. "But I'm the oldest."

"I understand Yvonne, but your brother and sister need a bigger room since they are sharing."

"It's not fair. They won't even take care of it. I mean, look at them now. They're running and ripping through the house like animals in a zoo. You *know* I would take care of my room. Mom, *please?*" I begged, but it didn't matter.

After a few minutes of feeling sorry for myself, I accepted my reality. At least we had a home, so what if my room was the smallest. I'll make it cozy and cover the walls with pictures of Joe. It was only right since I was the most obsessed fan of New Kids on the Block. When I shared my idea with my mom, she shot it down by saying, "You're not married to him, so you can't have his pictures up."

God help me! What planet was she on? I did it anyway.

CHAPTER TWENTY-THREE

I could see myself teaching the Quran. I could do this. I was capable of teaching a child how to write and recite. *It's in my blood.* The books Sister Mariam gave me were helpful. It wasn't my idea to teach like a scholar but in a simple manner. Finally settled in the house, I thought it was an appropriate time to begin working, plus, I could use the extra money. We agreed I would teach at her home which was conveniently near me. I also appreciated how I didn't have to spend much on gas. I started teaching the children once a week as soon as they came home from school. It bothered me that my children came back to an empty house, but I had to make ends meet.

It wasn't long before Sister Mariam saw how punctual and efficient I was in teaching her children that she told her friends all about me. I taught three more families based upon her gracious referrals. Before I knew it, I was invited to pray and read the Quran when Brothers and Sisters at the mosque had deaths in their families. It was all an honor. How proud would my grandfather be? Soon I would be asked to pray at various Quran Khanis where people were impressed by my ability to read two and a half parts of the Quran in one sitting. Dr. Azal, from the mosque, asked me to perform a wedding for one of his lawyer friends. Was this happening? Did it really take me divorcing Curtis to see what I could do for myself? I felt the old me coming back. Once more, I was a woman excited about the future, eager to learn, and walk with a high tide. Out of the utmost respect, I sought permission and guidance from Imam Ibrahimi to perform the wedding ceremony. I feared he would see it as a request out of my place since I was a woman. To my surprise, he directed me to go to the court in Rockville and file an application to begin the process. I couldn't believe the courts legally acknowledged me, a Muslim woman, as an official minister. I'm forever grateful for Imam Ibrahimi. When I performed my very first wedding, everybody was surprised to see me, a covered woman performing the marriage side by side with a priest. The bride was Iranian and the groom was American. During the reception, several progressive Americans approached me privately saying, "We've never seen this done before, we're so proud of you."

But it wasn't all roses and weddings. I would have to join others to complete the final rites of death: washing the body before burial. I never did any of this in my country. It was a little overwhelming. The hardest part? Well, that was it. I told myself that it was no more than being a doctor analyzing a body in the morgue.

And then there were the disappointments that came with teaching. I had an agreement with all of my parents that I was to be paid at the first of the month. Many parents abused my time. If there were five Saturdays in the month, they would just pay me for three Saturdays instead of all five. I couldn't believe it, they were doctors with money. It was pitiful how I would knock at their door and they chose to ignore me on top of not paying me on time. It broke my heart. If I were a man, I'm sure this wouldn't have happened. I had to constantly monitor my perspective on teaching: it was my life's joy to have the opportunity to teach each and every one of my students and watch them grow. Even still, I took the good with the bad and held my head high through it all.

After I saw how Yvonne decorated her room with this boy Joe all over her walls, I knew it was time to ground her in Islam. It was hard to do so before with all the turbulence in our lives. And as much as I didn't want to acknowledge it, watching her look like a twenty-one-year-old woman at age eleven made me quite uneasy and afraid. My friends often mistook her for being an adult. What was I supposed to do? She wasn't even a teenager yet and was already wearing a C cup. It was only a matter of time that she would seek the attention of boys or, worse, learn the power her body possessed to attract men. Several women from the mosque expressed interest in Yvonne marrying their sons, but she would only laugh in their faces, "Don't you *see*, I'm a *kid?*"

She didn't understand the serious nature of marriage. Back home, women were running families at her age. Yes, she was a child, but how was I to know she hadn't already kissed a boy? Just the other day I overheard her talking on the telephone to one of her friends about a first kiss. I thought I almost had a heart attack. Was kissing the least of my worries? Was she pregnant? And then the image of my daughter with a budding belling came to my mind. I went to her room and bust the door open. She didn't care. She sat on her bed, with the phone close to her ear.

"You kissed somebody!! I'm training you to be a respectful young lady and you're kissing a *boy?* Whore! How many times do I have to tell you? You aren't even married yet!"

Yvonne didn't respond. I could see she put the phone down. For once, did she have the decency to be ashamed of her behavior?

"You *will* be Muslim. My friends see you as loose, wild, out of control, an absolute disease! I'm here teaching the Quran and you want to be a *whore? Oh, Allah, you gave her to me and it's You who must take her away.*" I looked at Yvonne again with disgust. "I wish you were dead. No daughter of mine is going to be a slut and kiss boys. Do you want to be like those dirty girls on Donahue? "

I couldn't tell if she was shocked or was displaying a threatening sort of aloofness, but then she ran out of the room in tears and didn't speak to me all night long. I hung up the phone and went on to numb my brain with TV. Surely bigger things were going on in the world outside of my life with a hormonal daughter. And what do you know was the lead story on the 5 o'clock news? *The rise of teenage pregnancy.*

The next morning I called the mosque to learn about possible programs for Yvonne. The Imam told me about a weekend Muslim youth camp held in a hotel in Rockville. He put my mind at ease when he said, "It's a strict camp that followed a strong moral code including the separation of boys from the girls. Upon arrival, children get all of the rules: boys on one side of the hotel, girls on the other. Girls must remain covered at all times."

I enrolled her in the camp. Now, she would have no choice but to stay on the straight and narrow path, attract a sweet Muslim boy, and get married. This business of worshipping a boy on her wall and kissing someone was unacceptable. I had to get a hold of this problem before it got worse.

CHAPTER TWENTY-FOUR

Covering my head at camp was *not* a problem. With my bangs show-ing, I knew I was fly. I made it work. My hijab was on in such a way as to highlight the hoop earrings that my mom had recently bought me from Hecht's.

During the first lecture, I made eye contact with a green-eyed boy. He looked like he was about eighteen. I was drawn to him and knew he was aware of me too. We couldn't stop looking at each other. It was as if the very thing that was supposed to suppress us, the hijabs and the separation of boys and girls, was what excited me the most. I was curious to know what he'd think of me if he saw my hair. If he couldn't take his eyes off me with my head covered, then I was sure to blow his mind with what I had underneath. At break time, he slipped me a note. It said, "I want to see your hair. I know it's pretty, like you."

I responded with a note of my own, "Go to the playground during lunch." An excitement unlike no other came to me and it felt like a rush. I felt like I had power. Control. "You'll see me at the balcony of my room."

＊

With Yvonne at camp and the other two kids visiting their father, I finally enjoyed some time alone. I cleaned the house, enjoyed peace and quiet, and organized the books on the shelves in my study. In the midst of this, my eyes fell upon an unfamiliar book. When I opened it, it turned out to be a thick folder with several sheets of paper stapled together. The cover said "6th Grade Journal Entries for Mr. Henry's Class." I went through the pages and saw a series of letters between Yvonne and her teacher. Grabbing a cup of tea, I got comfortable in my recliner and prepared to read. Once I started reading the letters, I was unable to put them down. The line that haunted me most was when Yvonne wrote, " I can't believe I no longer have a home." And for the first time, I saw our life through my daughter's eyes.

I had been so busy surviving and getting through each day that I neglected her suffering I put the book down. Checking the time, I grabbed for my pocketbook and headed to the camp. The urge to wrap my arms around my daughter and assure her that everything was going to be fine came through me like a strong force. I'll convince her that life would get better and that I did it all for her. I'll let her know that I was going to be the mother she needed. So alive with a new understanding of my child, I walked faster, smiled while driving, and listened to music instead of the news on the radio. Cruising down I-270, the only thought on my mind was embracing Yvonne, my poor daughter who was crying out for help. Then, I pulled into the parking lot of the hotel, lowered the volume of the music, and drove the car into a space.

I took the key out of the ignition and reached for my pocketbook on the floor of the passenger seat. It was a little chilly outside when I realized I had left my coat at home. Then my eyes fell upon a scene: from a third-story balcony, a girl removed her headscarf revealing her long dark curly hair. It swayed from side to side like in the Clairol commercials. The girl stood at the balcony like Rapunzel, but it was clear she didn't need rescuing. In fact, she was putting on a show. It was apparent, even from the distance of my car that a seduction was occurring. A young boy in baggy pants couldn't take his eyes off my daughter.

ACKNOWLEDGEMENTS

This book becomes a reality with the kind of support and help of many individuals. I would like to extend my sincere thanks to all of them.

Foremost, I want to offer this endeavor to God for the wisdom he bestowed upon me, the strength, peace of mind and good health in order to see this work to completion.

I wish to express my sincerest gratitude for the support and love of my family: Neville Adams, the father of our children, we are no longer *Chasing Rainbows*- we *are* the Rainbow. To Layla and Samira, I do it all for you. To my extended family—the late Sheila Jacobs, my foster mother and her family, Pam and her family spanning from New York to Chesapeake, VA and the Baker/Braxton family, Brandon Gerald, and Jenny Trinh. They all kept me going, and this book would not have been possible without them.

To the pioneers of the Iranian Diaspora, I am forever in debt to you paving the way making it possible for me to have a voice. Special mention to Jasmin Darznik, Marjan Kamali, Persis Karim, Porochista Khakpoor, Nahid Rachlin, Soraya Shalforoosh, and Sholeh Wolpe.

To my first believers, Farhad Etminan, Mary Kay Jordan, Dwayne Parks, and Marjorie Smith —each of you lit a spark that never went out.

I wish to thank Montgomery College and University of Maryland's English Department for celebrating and documenting my journey. I would like to extend my sincere thanks to Professor Zita Nunes, Professor David Wyatt, and fellow Terp, Jason Reynolds for recognizing the importance of the immigrant/first generation narrative and encouraging me along.

Many thanks to the Toni Morrison Society, especially the Language Matters II teachers. Special thanks to Tonya Abari for being my academic partner in crime, Lori Stussie, for telling me on the bus what the title should be, Marceline Rogers, for our time in Princeton, Mekeiya Morrow, for her unwavering support, Frazier O'Leary, for his one-of-a-kind guidance through the world of Morrison and last but not least, Dr. Maryemma Graham for getting us all together. My time at Northern Kentucky University was life-changing and affirming.

To Toni Morrison, your work has inspired me to honor the story that has lived with me for so long. When I've thought about giving up, I think of your strength, grace, and dignity. I will continue to grow my daughters in your stories. To Edwidge Danticat, thank you for teaching us how to grieve. I have wept many times to your song.

I am grateful for a number of friends and colleagues in encouraging me to start the work, persevere with it, and finally to publish it. To my writer friends: Van Garrett, Tracye McQuirter, and Pamela Vines, your help through the years has enabled me to progress forward. To the Maryland Writers Project teachers, Joseph Mc Caleb, Patricia Stock, and Sylvia Robinson-Tibbs for inspiring educators to own their voice. To my Parkdale High School family, Brenda Barnes, Ericka Bullock, Charlena Carney, Dalitso Chinkhota, Christina Donnelly, Shasha Lowe, Eric Pavlat, Kathy Scarborough, Shayne Swift, Stephanie Weber, and Karen Venerable-Croft: my novel writing started with you. To Lyrikal Storm alumni, Ivan Alemanji, Joseph Ford, and Patrick Matam (Pages): your poetry and prayers stay with me. To my dear friend Silvia Alonso, there is only *one* you. To the Anthony Bowen YMCA staff and Bianca Moskaitis: thank you for providing me with a writing space. To Emily Arden with ReCreate a Space Perry Street: thank you for cultivating an environment for my creativity to thrive. To Amber Almonde, our time at the Mother's Love Gallery gave me hope to push forward.

To Sheila Gart, Dr. Robert Hunt, Razia Kosi, and Dr. Judith Upshaw: for your unwavering care and contribution to my mental health and healing. To Amber Khan, The Quietest Revolution, and my life coach, Steve Picante for guiding me to stand in my truth.

To my brother from another mother, Michael Twitty, it was an honor to be invited on your AWP panel in Washington, DC. Because of you, I met Garrard Conley and had the pleasure to workshop my story in the middle of nowhere in Pennsylvania with Garrard, Suz Carter, Joshua Dupree, Alexa Garvoille, Leah Haycock, and Mordecai Walfish. The insight I received on my book was invaluable. The poetic elements incorporated throughout the narrative exist because of Garrard's insistence.

To Colin Boyd Shafer, founder of *Finding American: Stories of Immigration* for memorializing my mother's immigrant experience. It was one of the proudest moments of her life, and we are honored for your time and work.

For valuable help in the preparation of the manuscript, I would like to thank Sarah Arbuthnot and Barbara Esstman for critical and helpful comments on early drafts. To my writers group members: Joel Breman, Kay Drew, Sydney Frymire, Andrea Jerrell, Kate Lemery, Marat Moore, Naomi Weiss, for their editorial help, keen insight, and ongoing support in bringing my stories to life. It is because of their efforts and dedication that I have a legacy to pass on to my family where one didn't exist before.

To Gene Cobb and Kris Peters, your contributions at the onset of my vision set me up for success. For assistance in the final stages of preparation, many thanks go to Heather Curran and Brandie Williams for final edits, to Luciano Emilio for the concept of the book cover, and Sanam Gouloubandi for translation assistance.

To all of the courageous participants of the *Crying Girl Movement:* your inner strength affirms the infinite possibilities that exist when we speak our truth. Your courage has sustained me through the years of my work. I thank each and every one of you: Sylvia Anderson, Livia

Abramoff, Brittani Ayer, Zakia Baker, Patrice Belton, Crystal Brandon, Jazmine Brazier, Ashley Brown, Tuesday Brown, Rocher Bubbitt, Alexis Burnette, Alexis Cambell, Joneka Chambers, London Chavis, Hazel Cherry, Henrietta Correa, Towanda Daniels, Kadiatu Diallo, Don Elliot, Cici Felton, Aja Finger, Tracy Fink, De'Ja Freeman, Nicole Gamble, Bonnie Goodwin, Amina Hamid, Isai Hamid, Cecilia Harley, Elizabeth Hartzel, Jewell Hill, Jordan Hill, Catherine A. Hinton, Jasmine Ikard, Chanae Issac, Ally Jackson, Nichole Jackson, Brittany Jiles, B. Lanae Johnson, Tameka Johnson, Brianna Jones, Christina Jones, Christy Jones, Sawa Kamara, Kamaren Kelton, Eileen King, Sixx Lee, Shannon Lewis, Dana Loveday, Jacqueline Lumax, Ann-Marie Maloney, Chant'l Martin, Kadijah S.P Mayo, Yolanda McCall, Devon Meriweather, Taice Mills, Jiffy Morales, Bianca Moskaitis, Essence Nelson, Ashley Nsangou, Monique Ogburn, Shayla Owens, Awura Osei, Demi Pedley, Shaneka Peters and family, Marcus Poston, Kandis Prather, Shante Ramos, Natalie Rodriguez, Victoria Sari, Courtney Samsky, Kenisha Samuels, Charletta Sinccoy, Star Snead, Kadijah Tall, Auriel Tate, Jenna Taylor, Amara Tek, Robin Thomas, Sophia Thompson, Jenny Trinh, Chantell Turner, Sally B. Walker, Amya Walters, Pamela Walters-Butts, Deandra Whyte, Janelle Wilfong, Brittany Williams, Katrina Woodridge, Allison Wright, and Nakisha Yates

To the individuals who strengthened me during the final stretch of the book's completion: Vicki Axarlis, Becky and Clay Harris, Tameka Hill and Family, Minister Yvette Gandy, Nefertiti Holland, Tamara Holland, Faisal Islam family, Yazmin Khan, Christy and Morris Jones, Keisha Kemp, Fajr Majeed Family, Emma Rahman, Iman Romodan and family, Qadri Family, Jasmine Reeder, Tanveer Shah family, and René Tsakounis—thank you.

Made in the USA
Monee, IL
10 February 2020

21585936R00134